GRAND CORPORATE STRATEGY AND CRITICAL FUNCTIONS

GRAND CORPORATE STRATEGY AND CRITICAL FUNCTIONS

Interactive Effects of
Organizational Dimensions

**Kyamas A. Palia
Michael A. Hitt
R. Duane Ireland
Yezdi H. Godiwalla**

PRAEGER

PRAEGER SPECIAL STUDIES • PRAEGER SCIENTIFIC

658,4
G 751

Library of Congress Cataloging in Publication Data

Main entry under title:
Organizational strategic functions.

Bibliography: p.
Includes index.
1. Organization.   2. Organizational
effectiveness.   3. Decision-making.
I. Palia, Kyamas A.
HD31.0759   658.4'012   82-430
ISBN 0-03-061734-0   AACR2

Published in 1982 by Praeger Publishers
CBS Educational and Professional Publishing
a Division of CBS Inc.
521 Fifth Avenue, New York, New York 10175 U.S.A.

© 1982 by Praeger Publishers

123456789   052   987654321

Printed in the United States of America

To our families

ACKNOWLEDGMENTS

The authors are grateful to the many people who have helped in this study. We acknowledge the patient and wise guidance of Wayne A. Meinhart and the statistical help of William D. Warde, both of Oklahoma State University. They have provided considerable input in various aspects of the study. We acknowledge the wisdom and specific skills provided by them in the various phases of this study.

Our thanks are also extended to Rudolph W. Trenton, Dale Armstrong, and Jackson F. Jackson for their suggestions.

We are grateful for the research and other support provided to us by our universities: the Oklahoma State University and the University of Wisconsin-Whitewater.

We acknowledge the many busy corporate executives who provided us the data utilized in this research study.

CONTENTS

LIST OF TABLES

xv

LIST OF FIGURES

LIST OF ACRONYMS

AOV	analysis of variance
CEO	chief executive officer
ERD	engineering and research and development
FIN	finance
GADM	general administration
GCS	grand corporate strategy
HSD	honestly significant difference
LSD	least significant difference
MKTG	marketing
PERS	personnel
PEU	perceived environmental uncertainty
PGR	public and government relations
PROD	production/operations
R&D	research and development
ROI	return on investment

1

INTRODUCTION

Wisdom is the ability to see the long-run consequences
of current actions, the willingness to sacrifice short-
run gains for larger long-run benefits, and the ability
to control what is controllable and not to fret over what
is not. Therefore the essence of wisdom is concern
with the future. It is not the type of concern with the
future that the fortune teller has; he only tries to predict it. The wise man tries to control it. Planning is
the design of a desired future and of effective ways of
bringing it about.

Russell L. Ackoff

Thinking well is wise; planning well, wiser; doing well
wisest and best of all.

Persian proverb

NATURE AND OBJECTIVES OF THE STUDY

Good analysis, planning, and organized management can help
an organization to be successful in achieving its objectives. This
business policy and corporate strategy[1] book is about issues that
have major impacts on the implementation of grand corporate strategy and emphasizes the importance of proper planning and implementation. It is based upon the perceptions and reports of top-level executives who are involved in the implementation of corporate strategies. The insights and wisdom of the practicing executives have
helped to provide verisimilitude to the concepts, discussions, and
conclusions presented in this study. The study analyzes a firm's
functional management (general administration, production, finance,

1

and so on) in the context of a firm's characteristics and its stated grand corporate strategy. The approaches adopted in the study are the overall organizational approach and the functional management influence-mix approach.[2] The study investigates the impact of different grand corporate strategies (stability, internal growth, external acquisitive growth, and retrenchment) on the types of organizational functions emphasized by firms.

This business policy and corporate strategy study examines the nature of relationships between the grand corporate strategies pursued by industrial firms and their top managers' perceptions of the relative importance (for effective strategy implementation) of different functional tasks. It also examines the nature of influence of size, corporate diversity, industry type, production system, organizational structure, and perceived environmental uncertainty on the interrelationships between the grand corporate strategies pursued and the relative importance of different functional tasks.

The field of business policy deals with the management of the total organization, and, therefore, it constitutes the heartland of business, business practice, and the management process. Because the study of corporate strategy is abstract and is in an embryonic stage, a predictive theory of business policy has not been developed and most of the research in this area has not been rigorous. This study attempts to provide new insights on the issues involving the effective implementation of grand corporate strategies in different types of industrial firms.

This study focuses upon top managers' perceptions—rather than objective observations of real world actions and results—of the relative importance of key result areas in different organizational functions for the effective implementation of different grand corporate strategies. It seeks to identify critical or strategically significant functions for effective implementation of each type of grand corporate strategy. The scope of this study is specific and limited to this end. Only the influence of organizational functions on corporate strategy implementation is examined; their influence on the formulation and evaluation of corporate strategy is not examined.

The field of business policy focuses on the total organization and deals with top management problems and functions. Any business policy phenomenon can involve a vast array of variables. Most of these variables are difficult to isolate, define, and measure. Omniscient human rationality is conspicuous by its absence in the field of business policy. In fact, even in the specifically narrow area of implementing the corporate strategy, Steiner and Miner (1977) point out that "the scope of managerial activities associated with implementation is virtually co-extensive with the entire process of management" (pp. 607-08). According to Mintzberg (1977) large corporation "research shows that most work processes of senior managers are unstructured and that they require a profound integration of various aspects of the organization and its environment."

It is difficult to establish accurate cause and effect relationships in a business policy study. The independent and dependent variables are generally influenced by a number of mediating or intervening variables. The major variables should not be ignored, as this will make the study too simplistic and unrealistic. At the same time, care should be taken that we do not include too many variables, otherwise the study would become unwieldy and infeasible. Thus, this study examines the influence of six key mediating variables: size, corporate diversity, industry, production system, organizational structure, and perceived environmental uncertainty. It is judged that these variables should be included because they are thought to be important to the grand corporate strategy of a firm.

The main objective of this study is to profile the relative strategic significance of seven different organizational functions for effective implementation of different grand corporate strategies, as perceived by the senior executives of large U.S. industrial corporations. This study utilizes the approach of functional areas' strategic significance-mix to the study of some of the problems involved in the implementation of grand corporate strategy. An astute and judicious determination of strategic key result areas in different functional tasks during the corporate strategy-formulation stage considerably facilitates the process of strategy implementation. In other words, the concept of "management by exception" of key result areas is operationalized, and top management attention is focused more on key result areas in the functional task(s), identified as critical or strategically significant to effective implementation of the grand corporate strategy pursued by the firm.

The study seeks answers to the following questions: Is it possible to identify the strategic mixes of organizational functions for effective implementation of different grand corporate strategies? Do the strategic mixes of organizational functions for a particular grand corporate strategy vary among companies of different size? among industries? among companies having different production systems? among companies having different organizational structures? and among companies with dissimilar managerial perceptions of environmental uncertainty?

Answers to these two main research questions have been derived through a field study, involving questionnaires mailed to the Fortune 1,000 industrial giants. To help focus the research, a conceptual framework was developed (see Figure 1.1).

FIGURE 1.1

The Study's Conceptual Framework

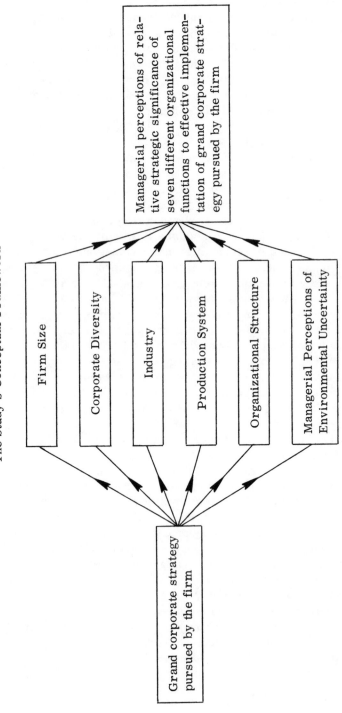

Source: Compiled by the authors.

4

SIGNIFICANCE OF THE STUDY

This research contributes to the development of the business policy area and furthers the progress of a more predictive field of study. Since the functional tasks' strategic significance-mix approach to the study of effective implementation of different grand corporate strategies is rather new, this study is primarily exploratory in nature. It builds upon the existing research and develops and empirically tests a coherent body of concepts.

The contingency approach of this study strikes a middle ground between the traditional universalistic approach of prescriptive theories and the particularistic case-study approach usually devoid of strong conceptual frameworks. It recognizes that the concept of corporate strategy is dynamic and complex and "suggests that there are definable patterns of relationships for different types of organizations and that we can improve our understanding of how the relevant variables interact" (Kast and Rosenzweig 1973, p. ix).

The increased use of an empirical approach to the study of business policy is all the more desirable since management researchers have tended to avoid this area of business policy. Although these problems are the most important to business organizations throughout the world, the pertinent variables cannot always be rigorously measured. Therefore, the research in this area typically is methodologically less elegant than in other more developed fields. Halpin (1968) wonders whether the social scientists have "the courage to study what is really worth studying" (p. 308). Mintzberg (1977) points out that

> researchers in management policy cannot use the most
> popular methodologies of other fields of management as
> models in their work. Their research must be related
> to the real world it purports to describe and be less ob-
> sessed with rigor as an end in itself. . . . Only by re-
> maining open to the rich complexity of reality can ef-
> fective theory-building be initiated in a new field.
> [P. 94]

As mentioned earlier, this study is exploratory in nature and is intended to reveal more fully the relationships between the variables involved. The exploratory type of study "seeks what is rather than predicts relations to be found"; such a study has

> three purposes: to discover significant variables in the
> field situation, to discover relations among variables
> and to lay the groundwork for later, more systematic

and rigorous testing of hypotheses. [Kerlinger 1973, p. 406]

Commenting on the usefulness of his research, Heau (1976) makes the following remarks which seem equally applicable to this study:

Research in business, as in any other social science, is not an end in itself, and the value of research is measured by its usefulness. In so far as a theory should possess the following attributes: explicability, generalisability, replicability and predictability, the present research is not a theory. Its aim is to provide an understanding, rather than to generate generalizations, allow replicative results or predict causality. Yet, Aristotle has remarked that an educated man demands no more than the exactitude that is allowed by the subject matter that is dealt with. [P. 7]

The study also provides contributions to effective management practice. It does not attempt to indulge in simplistic and premature prescriptions, but it does give the practitioners new insights into corporate strategies. However, by profiling the relative strategic significance of different functional tasks for effective implementation of different grand corporate strategies, based on a collective perception of practicing managers, it lays the foundation for a systematic evaluation of this concept for effective theory building and better management practice.

OUTLINE OF THE STUDY

This study is organized into seven chapters. This chapter has described the nature and objectives of the study and its significance to theory and practice.

Chapter 2 provides a review of the pertinent literature, both theoretical and empirical, from business policy and organization theory, which provides a foundation for the conceptual framework developed in this study.

Chapter 3 presents the definitions and operational measures of variables involved in the study.

Chapter 4 describes the conceptual framework which the study is designed to investigate. The general relationships among the theoretical and empirical works supporting the study and the research questions investigated by the study are posed and discussed.

Chapter 5 describes the research methodology used in the study.
Chapter 6 provides the analyses of data collected for the study.

Chapter 7 provides a summary and discussion of the major findings, discusses their implications for theory and management practice, and presents final conclusions.

NOTES

1. Like most emerging fields of study, the field of policy strategy has its own share of semantic problems and confusion. There are many different definitions of terms used by various distinguished scholars. There is a lack of consensus about the meaning of words like strategy and policy. These words have a long established meaning in common parlance, and they seem to change meaning with new developments. It is, however, important to distinguish between strategy and policy. According to Haner (1976), "A strategy is a multiple-step approach to achieve a specific objective. It is controlled by a plan, involves coordinated use of selected components and resources of the company, and covers the time frame necessary to accomplish the objective" (p. 259). "A policy," Haner says, "is a statement verbal, written or implied, of those principles and rules that are set by managerial leadership as guidelines and constraints for organizational thought and action" (p. 53). As a distinct discipline, the field of business policy lacks a common and universally accepted name, although strategic management seems to be currently very popular. For instance, according to Glueck and Willis (1979), "Strategic management and business policy is the portion of management theory concerned with top management decisions affecting the future of the total enterprise" (p. 95). It is interesting to note that the Academy of Management's professional division in this field is still known as the "Business Policy and Planning Division." In the business world, however, the terms strategic planning and corporate planning are more common. (For an extended discussion of this subject, see Steiner and Miner [1977, pt. 1].)

2. Godiwalla, Meinhart, and Warde (1979) have developed a functional influence-mix approach to the study of corporate strategy. They have analyzed the reported perceptions of chief executive officers of industrial organizations in portraying the nature of influence of functional management strategies upon the firm's overall corporate strategy.

2

REVIEW OF
RELATED
LITERATURE

INTRODUCTION

Empirical research in corporate strategy is in its infancy. As Hofer (1975) points out, "Since the concept of strategy was not developed extensively in the business literature until the late 1950s, almost no empirical research related to it was done until the early 1960s" (p. 790). During the past two decades various empirical research studies have been directed toward the theoretical development of the concept of corporate strategy.

This chapter broadly reviews important concepts in the field of business policy and organization theory that are directly relevant to the development of this study's conceptual framework discussed later in Chapter 4. Within this chapter relevant parts of three major areas of literature are surveyed: corporate strategy, the relative importance of different organizational functions, and contextual variables—environment, technology, size, and structure.

CORPORATE STRATEGY

Scholars have provided similar definitions of corporate strategy. Alfred Chandler (1962), in his seminal work Strategy and Structure: Chapters in the History of American Industrial Enterprise, defines strategy as "the determination of the basic long-term goals and objectives of an enterprise, and the adoption of courses of action and the allocation of resources necessary for carrying out these goals" (p. 13).

Quinn defines a strategy "as a plan that determines how the organization can best achieve its desired ends in light of the opposing pressures exerted by competition and by its own limited resources" (Gilmore and Brandenburg 1962, p. 68).

Glueck (1976) defines strategy as "a unified, comprehensive, and integrated plan designed to assure that the basic objectives of the enterprise are achieved" (p. 3).

Corporate strategy, therefore, refers to an organization's master plan for achieving its mission, objectives, and goals. "Strategy indicates how the organization plans to get where it wants to go" (Thompson and Strickland 1978, p. 12). It is clear that developing and sustaining an ongoing strategy is extremely vital to the long-range viability of the organization, because it determines the major directions the organization takes and the momentum with which it moves.

Other scholars provide a more comprehensive definition of corporate strategy. Aguilar (1967) offers the following:

> Company strategy is an integrated and harmonious pattern of objectives which are of fundamental importance to the long-term survival and health of a company. As such, strategy defines the company's basic image, purposes, fields of present and future activity, and expected future position in these fields. Strategy should be responsive to both the external environment and the strengths and weaknesses—present and potential—within the firm itself. [P. 4]

Steiner (1969b) believes that

> developing a strategy is usually a very difficult and fateful task. It usually means questioning old methods, exploring unfamiliar environmental waters, facing up to an objective evaluation of strengths and weaknesses, forcing important changes on people in the firm and organizational arrangements, and taking high risks with the firm's capital. This has to be done in a world of rapid change, and it has to be done continuously. [Pp. 238-39]

Textbook wisdom suggests that

> ideally, every corporate body has a strategy that meets three criteria: (1) It recognizes and understands how the forces of the past have affected the organization. (2) It is responsive to the current forces of change. (3) It is capable of implementing programs based on the first two considerations. [Vance 1970, p. 6]

As Tilles (1963) notes, "While the notion of a strategy is extremely easy to grasp, working out an agreed-upon statement for a given company can be a fundamental contribution to the organization's future success" (p. 112).

Jauch and Osborn (1981) define strategy as the combination or profile of environmental, contextual, and structural elements affecting an organization at any given time. When the unit of analysis is the entire organization, then strategy is defined as the profile of overall environmental, contextual, and structural complexity (pp. 491-98).

The aforementioned definitions of corporate strategy highlight two important dimensions: scope and importance. Corporate strategy, so defined, refers to a master strategy, a grand strategy, or an overall strategy and encompasses "the entire pattern of a company's basic mission, purposes, objectives, policies, and specific resource deployment" (Steiner and Miner 1977, p. 20). Paine and Naumes (1974) distinguish an overall or grand strategy from different corporate strategies in the following manner:

> An overall strategy may be defined as a plan which encompasses not only the mission, policies, objectives and more specific goals of the organization, but also a plan of action for achieving these objectives and goals. Subsequent decisions are based on the plan. On the other hand corporate strategies may be described as a stream of significant decisions which emerge over a period of time into a pattern. In this case the decisions, made on an ad hoc basis while trying to adapt to various uncertainties, determine the strategy. [P. 7; emphasis added]

According to Newman (1967), "a firm's success depends on its basic plan—its master strategy—for dealing with the elements of change, growth, and adaptation" (p. 77). Robert E. Wood, while chairman of the board of Sears Roebuck and Company, once commented: "Business is like war in one respect, if its grand strategy is correct, any number of tactical errors can be made and yet the enterprise proves successful" (Chandler 1962, p. 235). As military strategists know, in any war if the overall strategy is right and effective, an ultimate victory can be achieved in spite of some setbacks in a few battles.

In the business policy literature few attempts have been made to provide an exhaustive scheme of classification of grand corporate strategies. Glueck (1976, pp. 120-21) provides a four-way classification of grand corporate strategies:

1. Stability (most frequently used)
2. Growth
3. Retrenchment (least frequently used)
4. Combination (of two or more grand strategies, either simultaneously or sequentially)

Of the grand corporate strategies listed above, growth and retrenchment strategies have been subjected to further analysis and classification by many authors. There are other types of strategies that may be mentioned here. There are product-market strategies at the business and/or division levels; these have been analyzed in detail. Strategies in different functional areas have also been described and analyzed. The analysis of one type of grand corporate strategy—external acquisitive growth—will be discussed in this section, since it highlights the importance of different organizational functions in different types of external-acquisitive-growth strategies.

Kitching (1967), in his study of corporate acquisitions, classified acquisitions into five different categories:

> Horizontal—Same industry as buying company, with approximately the same customers and suppliers.
> Vertical integration—Major supplier or customer of the buying company and in the same industry.
> Concentric marketing—Same customer types as buying company but different technology.
> Concentric technology—Same technology as buying company but different customer types.
> Conglomerate—Customers and technology different from those of buying company. [P. 85]

Howell (1970) believes that existing schemes of classifying acquisitions (for example, the Federal Trade Commission's horizontal, vertical, and conglomerate) often fail to recognize the intrinsic organizational implications of different types of acquisitions. He proposes the following classification scheme generated by isolating acquisition candidates along functional business dimensions:

1. Financial
2. Marketing
3. Manufacturing

Financial acquisition growth strategies are conglomeratic in nature with the primary focus on the financial implications of the acquisition. Marketing acquisition growth strategies are conglomeratic in nature with the primary focus on the marketing implications of the

TABLE 2.1

Summary of Major Differences between High-Performing Conglomerates and Vertically Integrated Firms

	Conglomerate Firms	Vertically Integrated Firms
Environmental requirements	Greater environmental diversity Higher environmental uncertainty Less complex required interdependence Less intensive internal funding requirements More uncertain patterns of funds flow	Lower environmental diversity Lower environmental uncertainty More complex required interdependence More intensive internal funding requirements More certain patterns of funds flow
Patterns of organizational choice	Higher degree of divisional self-containment Smaller headquarters units focusing mainly on policy issues Less complex integrative devices	Lower degree of divisional self-containment Larger headquarters units focusing on both policy and operating issues More complex integrative devices
Organizational states	Higher total differentiation Lower integrative effort Greater rapidity in responding to divisional requests Influence peaks at a lower (division general manager) level Performance evaluation systems with explicitly defined criteria, direct linkage between results and rewards and heavier emphasis on financial/end-result criteria	Lower total differentiation Higher integrative effort Less rapidity in responding to divisional requests Influence peaks at a higher (senior vice-president) level Performance evaluation systems that are more informally administered, without direct linkage between results and rewards, and balanced emphasis on financial/end-result and operating/intermediate criteria

Source: Stephen A. Allen III, "Management Issues in Multidivisional Firms," Sloan Management Review 13 (Spring 1972): 63.

12

acquisition. Manufacturing acquisition growth strategies are concentric technology in nature with the primary focus on the technological implications of the acquisition.

The firm's grand corporate strategy (both past and current) determines the nature of the firm's relevant environments and the resulting organizational states. In addition, it suggests the range of feasible options for the firm's organization and management. Table 2.1 summarizes the major differences Allen (1972) "found between the high performing conglomerates and vertically integrated companies with regard to environmental requirements, organizational choices, and resulting organizational states" (pp. 62-63).

Miles and Snow (1978) have developed a typology of organizations: "Each of these types has its own strategy for responding to the environment, and each has a particular configuration of technology, structure, and process that is consistent with its strategy" (p. 29). These types are the following:

1. Defenders tend to follow "stability" strategy and are risk-avert outside their narrow product-market domains.

2. Prospectors tend to pursue "growth" strategies and are perceived as risk takers.

3. Analyzers tend to be more cautious, risk-neutral, and balanced; seek a "strategic fit" or "common thread" between their existing and new product-market domains and pursue growth strategies in concentrically related areas.

4. Reactors do not pursue any of the above-mentioned strategies; lack any long-term strategy or an effective and consistent strategy-structure relationship; are in a state of perpetual instability and are characterized by "management by crisis."

Along with the different perspectives that have been provided in the definitions of corporate strategy or grand strategy, it is useful to also provide an indication about the nature of strategy formulation and the corporate planning process. It is through the process of strategic planning that a firm's objectives, goals, plans, and grand corporate strategy are formulated. Thus, grand corporate strategy is one of the important outputs of a firm's strategic planning process.

The strategic planning process may be defined as a continuous process of the search, analysis, and communication of all data and information utilized in all strategic decision making. Various authors have forwarded certain viewpoints about the ways strategic planning does or should progress. A few are briefly reviewed in the following passages.

Lorange (1980) identifies the four aspects of corporate strategic planning as the following:

Allocation of strategic resources (consisting of funds, managerial
    skills, technology, and know-how)
Adaptation (acquisition of new business or moving into new markets)
Integration
Management development

He states that strategic planning should be pursued at three levels in the following ways:

Corporate level: portfolio strategy
Divisional level: business strategy
Functional level: strategic programs

Kloeze, Molenkamp, and Roelofs (1980) contend that the positioning of strategic planning in an organization is very important. The rapid rate of change in the environment (whether caused by technological, economic, social, or political causes) gives the role of forward planning considerable importance. Furthermore, internal participation must be given adequate weight in such planning to avoid alienation problems.

RELATIVE IMPORTANCE OF DIFFERENT
ORGANIZATIONAL FUNCTIONS

Various research studies have been conducted to determine the relative importance of different functional tasks in different types of organizations. In one of the earliest studies of this kind Stevenson (1968) considered the organizational attributes as corporate strengths and weaknesses, and grouped them under five functional categories; the factors considered important at top management levels (presidents and board chairmen) were organizational (42.4 percent), personnel (32.9 percent), and financial (15.3 percent) (Glueck 1976, p. 91). Aguilar (1967, p. 43), in his study of the relative importance of different areas of external information, found that market tidings (marketing management's subenvironment) accounted for 58 percent of all responses, based on the responses from managers (39 percent of whom were among the high echelons of management). Steiner (1969a) tried to develop a profile of strategic factors in business success both for current performance and future importance. Glueck (1976) concludes from Steiner's study that "the crucial aspects of the strategy that need to be evaluated are: (1) Man-

FIGURE 2.1

The Manufacturing Cycle and Technology

Production System (that is, technology)	Manufacturing Cycle		
Unit and Small Batch	Marketing ⟶	**CRITICAL FUNCTION** Development ⟶	Production
Large Batch and Mass	Development ⟶	Production ⟶	Marketing
Process	Development ⟶	Marketing ⟶	Production

Note: The critical function is the one on which the cycle relies for success. These functions will be the most prestigious, and those who perform them will have high influence in the firm.

Source: Joan Woodward, Industrial Organization: Theory and Practice (New York: Oxford University Press, 1965). Reproduced from P. T. Terry, "Organizational Implications for Long Range Planning," Long Range Planning 8 (February 1975): 29, by permission of the author and the publisher. Copyright © 1965 by Oxford University Press.

agement quality and development, (2) Environmental appraisal, especially market tidings, and (3) Financial return" (p. 265).
Woodward (1965) studied the relationship between the type of production system (unit, mass, and process) and three organizational functions (development, production, and marketing). She concluded that firms having different production systems can be expected to have different "critical functions." Specifically, "There seemed to be

one function that was central and critical in that it had the greatest effect on success and survival" (p. 126). Figure 2.1 presents the manufacturing cycle and the critical function for each of the three types of production systems.

Lawrence and Lorsch (1967b) found "that marketing had more influence than production in both container-manufacturing and food-processing firms, apparently because of its involvement in (uncertain) innovation and with customers" (Hickson, Hinnings, Lee, Schneck, and Pennings 1971, p. 219).

Kitching (1967) investigated both the relative payoff values from synergy after acquisition and the ease with which synergy is released in each of the five business functions. The usual notions about potential for synergy indicate that business functions can be ranked in order of importance in the following manner:

1. Production
2. Technology (including research and development)
3. Marketing
4. Organization
5. Finance

However, Kitching's findings contradict the traditional notions. Far from producing the lowest payoff, finance had the highest payoff in all types of mergers except one—horizontal mergers—where marketing had the highest payoff, followed very closely by finance. Technology and production, on the other hand, produced the lowest relative payoff values from synergy after acquisition. Finance was also found to be the function in which it was easiest to release synergy in all types of mergers except one—concentric technology—where synergy was achieved with the greatest ease in the area of technology.

Kitching points out that his findings are subject to two major limitations. First, his sample dealt with companies acquired two to seven years ago, and it probably takes longer to realize production synergy than any other type. This might partly account for the low relative payoff values in production. Second, 45 percent of his sample constituted conglomerates, where, by definition, companies with dissimilar technological/production skills merge together. The characteristic also partly explains the lower relative payoff values assigned to the production function by the corporate executives. However, the most important conclusion of this study is that effective management of the finance function is very crucial to the success of mergers.

Many authors have noted the increasing importance of the finance function. With the increasing trend toward multiplant operations, the traditional argument of scale economies (resulting in lower costs and higher capital efficiency) does not seem valid even in the case of large, single, and dominant business firms. For large multi-industry and multinational conglomerates the only synergistic benefit arises from a possible financial synergy. This outcome indicates a noticeable trend toward an increase in direct involvement of the chief financial officers in the strategic issues handled by top management. Pohl (1973) points out the following:

> These two factors—taking the lead in resolving important issues of general concern to the company and working more closely with the major executives throughout the company—should enhance the financial executive's stature in the organization. In the United States, in fact, the financial executive has already become a favored contender for the chief executive's chair. According to two recent surveys, chief executive officers with financial background accounted for 24 percent of all CEO's in 1971, an increase from 15 percent in 1967. Moreover, of all CEO's appointed in 1971, about 33 percent had financial backgrounds, exceeding all other backgrounds by a wide margin. [See Figure 2.2]
> This trend, which does not seem to have reached its peak yet in the United States, is expected to gain momentum in Europe during the next few years as a result of the changing demands on the financial executive. It is a direct reflection of the important contribution the financial executive can and must make to his company in the years to come. [P. 22]

Fox (1973) (as quoted by Hofer 1975, pp. 790-91) studied the influence of the product life cycle on business strategies and on the importance of the appropriate functional policies. He identified a specific functional focus for each of the five stages of the product life cycle. For instance, he determined that during the "decline" stage of the product life cycle, the functional focus of the business strategy should be on finance. Hofer (1977, p. 7) also identified the major functional concern for each of the seven distinct stages of product-market evaluation.

Heau (1976) examined the relationship between strategy (defined in terms of product relatedness) and corporate structure. For this purpose the firms were grouped under four strategy categories: vertically integrated, technology diversifiers, market diversifiers, and conglomerates. According to Heau, a comparison of the four categories of firms along their corporate organizational structure would show the tendencies depicted in Table 2.2. Aside from showing the characteristics of organizational structure and information

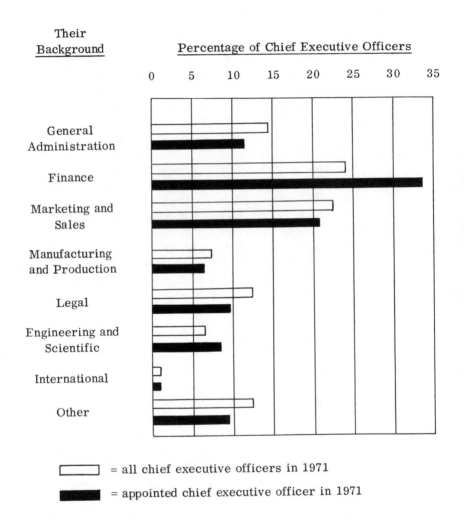

FIGURE 2.2

Shifts on the Way to the Top

Their
Background

Percentage of Chief Executive Officers

□ = all chief executive officers in 1971

■ = appointed chief executive officer in 1971

Source: Analysis of data published by Forbes (May 1972) on
724 largest U.S. corporations. The analysis was published in Management Practice (Summer 1972). Reproduced from Herman H.
Pohl, "The Coming Era of the Financial Executive," Business Horizons 16 (June 1973): 22, by permission of the author and the publisher. Copyright © 1972 by Forbes.

18

TABLE 2.2

Relationship between Strategy and Corporate Structure
(defined in terms of product relatedness)

Structure/Strategy	Vertically Integrated	Technology Diversifiers	Market Diversifiers	Conglomerates
Corporate structure				
1. Functions existing at the top (in addition to control, finance, legal, personnel)	Almost all	Research and development Engineering	Marketing Purchasing	None
2. Size of the corporate staff	Very large	Quite large	Quite large	Very small
3. Role of the group vice-president (if any)	Small	Optional	Optional	Essential
Information flow				
4. Dominant nature of information flow between corporation and divisions	Operational	Technology biased	Marketing biased	Financial
5. Amount of information between corporation and divisions	Very high	High	High	Low
Corporate culture				
6. Orientation of top management	Industry (capacity)	Technology	Marketing (market segmentation, market share)	Financial (product-market portfolio)

Source: Dominique G. Heau, "Long Range Planning in Divisionalized Firms: A Study of Corporate Divisional Relationships" (Ph.D. diss., Harvard Business School, 1976), p. 9.

19

flow for each category of firms, he also identified the corporate culture or the orientation of top management for each category. In terms of this study, the latter relationships could be restated as follows:

Growth Strategy	Critical Function
Vertical integration	Production/operations
Concentric technology diversification	Engineering and research and development
Concentric marketing diversification	Marketing
Conglomerate diversification	Finance

In a recent study of functional managements' influence on the overall corporate strategy, Godiwalla, Meinhart, and Warde (1979) found that for firms having a unit production system, marketing was the significantly strategic functional management. This outcome was also true for firms having mass manufacturing production systems, but for firms having a process type of production, marketing was found to be the critical strategic function, while finance was also found to be very important. For all the firms (of different sizes and production systems) taken together, marketing, finance, and production were found to be the three most influential functions.

Miles and Snow (1978), in their study of interindustry comparisons of strategy in electronics and food processing, developed the concept of "strategic function"; it "refers to those functional areas within the organization considered by members of the dominant coalition to be of strategic importance to successful competition in their industry" (p. 196). They found that the chief executives' perceptions of the top three strategic functions vital to their competitive success were different in the two industries.

Rockart (1979) discusses a new approach (called the critical success factor [CSF] method) to defining the managerial information needs; it is currently being actively researched and applied at the Center for Information Systems Research in the Sloan School of Management at Massachusetts Institute of Technology. According to Rockart, for any business, critical success factors are

the limited number of areas in which results, if they are satisfactory, will ensure successful competitive performance for the organization. They are the few key areas where "things must go right" for the business to flourish. If results in these areas are not adequate, the organization's efforts for the period will be less than de-

sired. . . . As a result the critical success factors are
areas of activity that should receive constant and care-
ful attention from management. The current state of
performance in each area should be continually measured, and that information should be made available.
[P. 85]

Formulation of functional strategies and plans often requires a
special skill, as it relates to certain functional areas. Frederick
(1981) observes about functional strategies that if their planning is
based upon incremental analysis, then such planning can overcome
weaknesses inherent in traditional comprehensive planning.

CONTEXTUAL VARIABLES: ENVIRONMENT, TECHNOLOGY, SIZE, AND STRUCTURE

This study also examines the nature of influence of size, corporate diversity, industry type, production system, organizational
structure, and perceived environmental uncertainty on the interrelationships between grand corporate strategies and the relative importance of different functional tasks. Accordingly, pertinent literature
relating to these contextual variables will be reviewed briefly in this
section.

Environment

Environment and Strategic Planning

Schendel and Hatten (1972) take a broader view of the emerging
discipline of business policy, a view they call strategic management.
An important characteristic of strategic management is its prime
concern with environmental change, its anticipation and adaption to it.
According to Schendel and Hatten,

Strategic Management is the managerial process of determining and maintaining a viable relationship between the
organization and its environment through the use of selected objectives, and efficient resource allocations to
major programs and policies. Strategic management
seeks a stable and viable match between the organization,
its needs and resources, and the demands imposed by
the environmental setting. [P. 100]

TABLE 2.3

Postulated Characteristics of Successful Strategic Managers

Aggressive	High tolerance for ambiguity and
Self-confident	frustration
Self-reliant and independent	Charismatic leadership ability
High achievement needs	Organizing skills
High initiative	Creative and imaginative
Persistent	Risk takers but not gamblers
Persuasive	Above-average intelligence
Extroverted	Self-learners
Flexible	Broad experience base with frequent
Receptive to change	initial specialization
	High energy level

Source: J. R. Rawls, D. J. Rawls, and R. Radosevich, "Identifying Strategic Managers," Business Horizons 18 (December 1975): 78.

Rawls, Rawls, and Radosevich (1975) also contend that strategic management is mainly concerned with relationships between the firm and its environment. Strategic managers have roles and functions that are different from those of the operations managers. Rawls, Rawls, and Radosevich reviewed the attributes of successful managers, entrepreneurs, and organizational innovators. They compiled a tentative list of the attributes of successful strategic managers (see Table 2.3).

In one of the earliest studies of environmental influences relevant to organizational planning, Dill (1958) examined the influence of environmental constraints on the structure of organizations and the behavior of organizational participants. He studied the influence of the structure of environment, the accessibility of information about environment, and the managerial perceptions of the meaning of environmental information on managerial autonomy. He concluded that "behavior depends on the patterns of inputs from the environment to an organization and on the interpretation of these inputs as taken by members of the organization" (p. 409).

Carter's (1971) research suggests "that the goals of an organization can be closely related to the degree of uncertainty in its general environment and to the uncertainty in a particular project's forecasts." He hypothesizes the relationship as follows: "The greater the uncertainty of outcome in the total environment of the organization, the greater the number of criteria, that is, goals, which will be sought to guide the strategic decisions" (p. 423).

In an exploratory study of the impact of the business environment on the long-range planning process, Lindsay and Rue (1978) found

> that large business firms in a variety of industries are attempting to "fit" their long-range planning processes to their perceived environmental conditions. That a number of the strategies used to achieve this "fit" are in line with concepts developed by organization theorists. [P. 119]

Their study also focused on the specifics of the boundary-spanning process of long-range planning, and the findings suggest "that environmental turbulence and firm size are important 'contingent variables' to consider in the design of an effective and efficient long-range planning process" (p. 119).

Since grand corporate strategy is formulated on the basis of organization-environment interactions, it must be consistent with the prevailing and anticipated environmental conditions. As Richards (1978) points out, "To be viable over long periods, the master strategy . . . must be viable in the light of the environmental conditions" (p. 32). Therefore, a change in the grand corporate strategy results mainly from actual or anticipated changes in the external environment (Hofer 1973). In a research study covering 358 companies over a 45-year period, Glueck (1976) tried to determine the challenges the companies were facing. He found broader or general environmental challenges to be the most important, followed by market challenges. Glueck offered the following proposition: "The major causes of growth, decline and other large-scale changes in firms are factors in the environment, not internal developments" (p. 48). Hofer and Schendel (1978) sum up the argument by stating that

> research by Hofer (1973) and Glueck (1976) indicates that almost all the strategic opportunities that a business will face stem from fundamental changes in the market and the industry in which it competes, its sources or conditions of supply, the action of its competitors, the broader environmental forces that have impact on these areas, or the ways that all of these factors interact with one another. [P. 110]

Since a firm's external environment is one of the major determinants of its corporate strategy, the inclusion of environmental variables in any research dealing with corporate strategy cannot be too strongly emphasized. Taylor (1973) therefore argues that strategic decisions are "concerned with effecting major changes in the 'linkages' between the enterprise and its environment" (p. 37).

Classification of Environments

Bourgeois (1980) notes that the strategy literature has long stressed the importance of scanning and searching the environment. He observes that when firms are operating in more dynamic and uncertain environments the managers perceive the strategies to be more comprehensive and multifaceted. The managers also tend to be more proactive and innovative.

In order to facilitate the process of scanning organizational environments, it is very useful to understand the different methods for classification of organizational environments. A study of environmental classification methods would help a strategist correctly search and scan organizational environments, and in doing so he would have a better and more realistic understanding of his firm's environments and what kind of grand corporate strategy would better serve his firm.

Duncan (1972) distinguished between an organization's internal and external environment and, based on his research, constructed a list of environmental components (Table 2.4) particularly relevant to industrial organizations. He conceptualized four different types of environments (as shown in Table 2.5): Simple-Static (Cell 1); Complex-Static (Cell 2); Simple-Dynamic (Cell 3); and Complex-Dynamic (Cell 4). He also hypothesized the degree of uncertainty that will be experienced by decision units in each of these four types of environments.

Environmental constraints, contingencies, opportunities, and problems affect the strategies, structure, and size of the organizations. The character of the environment determines the degree of pressure for change, the immediacy for change, and uncertainties facing the organization. Relatively placid environments, because of their predictability, permit varying organizational strategies. In contrast, turbulent environments are dynamic and are characterized by complex and rapidly changing conditions impinging on the organizations, which tend to increase uncertainty, reduce control, and make prediction more difficult (Terreberry 1968).

Emery and Trist (1965) developed a typology of environments in which the environments were seen as being causal for the organizations within them. The four types of environments were

Type

1   Placid, randomized
2   Placid, clustered

TABLE 2.4

Factors and Components Comprising the Organization's Internal and External
Environments

Internal environment
1. Organizational personnel component
    a. Educational and technological background and skills
    b. Previous technological and managerial skill
    c. Individual member's involvement and commitment to attaining sys-
       tem's goals
    d. Interpersonal behavior styles
    e. Availability of manpower for utilization within the system
2. Organizational functional and staff units component
    a. Technological characteristics of organizational units
    b. Interdependence of organizational units in carrying out their objec-
       tives
    c. Intraunit conflict among organizational functional and staff units
    d. Interunit conflict among organizational functional and staff units
3. Organizational level component
    a. Organizational objectives and goals
    b. Integrative process integrating individuals and groups into contributing
       maximally to attaining organizational goals
    c. Nature of the organization's product service

External environment
4. Customer component
    a. Distributors of product or service
    b. Actual users of product or service
5. Suppliers component
    a. New materials suppliers
    b. Equipment suppliers
    c. Product parts suppliers
    d. Labor supply
6. Competitor component
    a. Competitors for suppliers
    b. Competitors for customers
7. Sociopolitical component
    a. Government regulatory control over the industry
    b. Public political attitude toward industry·and its particular product
    c. Relationship with trade unions with jurisdiction in the organization
8. Technological component
    a. Meeting new technological requirements of own industry and related
       industries in production of product or service
    b. Improving and developing new products by implementing new techno-
       logical advances in the industry

Source: Robert B. Duncan, "Characteristics of Organizational Environments and Perceived Environmental Uncertainty," Administrative Science
Quarterly 17 (1972): 315.

25

TABLE 2.5

Environmental State Dimensions and Predicted Perceived Uncertainty Experienced by Individuals in Decision Units

	Simple	Complex
	Cell 1 (low perceived uncertainty)	Cell 2 (moderately low perceived uncertainty)
Static	1. Small number of factors and components in the environment 2. Factors and components are somewhat similar to one another 3. Factors and components remain basically the same and are not changing	1. Large number of factors and components in the environment 2. Factors and components are not similar to one another 3. Factors and components remain basically the same
	Cell 3 (moderately high perceived uncertainty)	Cell 4 (high perceived uncertainty)
Dynamic	1. Small number of factors and components in the environment 2. Factors and components are somewhat similar to one another 3. Factors and components of environment are in continual process of change	1. Large number of factors and components in the environment 2. Factors and components are not similar to one another 3. Factors and components of environment are in continual process of change

Source: Robert B. Duncan, "Characteristics of Organizational Environments and Perceived Environmental Uncertainty," Administrative Science Quarterly 17 (1972): 320.

3   Disturbed reactive
4   Turbulent field

Each of the aforementioned types affects the size, structure, and functioning of the organizations in different ways. For instance, the Type 4 environment is associated with greatly increased uncertainty owing to the highly complex and rapidly changing nature of the environment. Organizations facing such environments tend to be more R&D conscious. Public relations functions in such organizations also become increasingly important since organizations have to constantly struggle to seek and maintain social and economic legitimacy.

Burns and Stalker (1961) classified organizations into two polar extremes: mechanistic and organic. When the rate of technical and commercial change is high, organizations assume an organic form; the mechanistic organizational form is appropriate for stable conditions when the rate of technical and commercial change is low.

Thompson (1967) classified the organization's environment into four types: stable and homogeneous, stable and heterogeneous, unstable and homogeneous, and unstable and heterogeneous. He argued that heterogeneity and instability in the environment have significant implications for organizational structure.

Bourgeois (1980) explains in detail about the general environment and task environment. He notes that literature on organizational environments does not provide any clear resolution when it comes to objective versus perceived environmental conditions. Strategy literature appears to consider managerial perception about strategic organizational environments.

Organization-Environment Interaction

Hrebiniak (1978) very aptly sums up the gist of the main thesis of Lawrence and Lorsch's classic 1967 study.

> Degree of differentiation depends on the uncertainty facing the organization; the greater the uncertainty, the greater the organizational differentiation necessary to cope with external demands; the greater the differentiation (including both task and attitudinal differences), the greater the integration needed to insure goal-directed behavior. [Pp. 349-50]

Lorsch (1973), commenting further on the Lawrence and Lorsch study mentioned earlier, states that

> there must be a fit between internal organizational characteristics and external environmental requirements if

TABLE 2.6

Detailed Systems for Classifying Strategic Challenges and Responses

---

Strategic Challenges

Market-related challenges
1. Major changes in market structure
2. Major changes in the product life cycle
3. Major changes in demographic structure
4. Major changes in the types of customers served
5. Major changes in the price elasticity of demand
6. Major increases in total demand (other than above)
7. Stagnation of or major decreases in total demand (other than above)

Industry-related challenges
1. Major changes in the nature of product differentiation
2. Major changes in the economies of scale
3. Major changes in the price/cost structure
4. Major changes in product or process technology
5. Major changes in the distribution system
6. Major change in barriers to entry (other than above)

Competitor-related challenges
1. Entry of new competitors
2. Exit of old competitors
3. Major changes in the market share of existing competitors

Supplier-related challenges
1. Major changes in the availability of raw materials
2. Major changes in the conditions of trade
3. Entry of new suppliers or exit of old suppliers

Resource- and capability-related challenges
1. Major excess of capital or cash flow
2. Major shortage of capital or inadequate cash flow
3. Major threat of outside takeover
4. Major excess of production facilities
5. Major inadequacy or sudden loss of production facilities
6. Major inadequacy or loss of top management

Broader environmental challenges
1. Major changes in economic conditions
2. Major changes in political/legal constraints
3. Major changes in social/cultural values

Changes in objectives
1. Change growth objectives
2. Change profitability objectives
3. Change other objectives

Changes in strategy
1. Major expansion in product market scope
    a. Increase penetration
    b. New markets/existing products
    c. New products/existing markets/existing needs
    d. New products/existing markets/different needs
    e. Forward integration
    f. Backward integration
    g. Concentric diversification: marketing
    h. Concentric diversification: production
    i. Conglomerate diversification
2. Major contraction of product/market scope
    a. Major contraction of market coverage
    b. Major contraction of product line
3. Major expansion of geographic scope
4. Major contraction of geographic scope
5. Major changes in distinctive competences
    a. Major increase in marketing competence
    b. Major improvement in distribution capability
    c. Major increase in production competence
    d. Major increase in R&D competence
    e. Major increase in financial capability
    f. Major increase in managerial competence

Change functional policies

Liquidation
1. Liquidation of product line
2. Liquidation of division
3. Liquidation of corporation

No response

Source: Charles W. Hofer, "Some Preliminary Research on Patterns of Strategic Behavior," Academy of Management Proceedings, 1973, p. 48.

the organization is to perform effectively in dealing with its environment. This fit between an organization and its environment, as we have examined it, has two related aspects. First, each functional unit (e.g. sales, production, and research) must have internal characteristics consistent with the demands of its particular sector of the total environment. . . . The second aspect of the organization-environment relationship which we have found to be important is that the total organization must achieve, in spite of the differentiation among its units, the pattern of integration required by the total environment. [P. 132]

The latter aspect stresses the importance of the general administration role and functions at the corporate level.

Hofer (1973) believes that

in general, the leading authors in the field—Andrews, Ansoff, Cannon, Ewing, Guth, Katz, McNichols, Newman, and Tilles—agree that strategic planning is concerned with the development of a viable match between the opportunities and risks present in the external environment and the organization's capabilities and resources for exploiting these opportunities. [P. 47]

Hofer (1973), for his preliminary research on patterns of strategic behavior, developed detailed systems for classifying strategic challenges and responses under different sets of categories (Table 2.6). A closer examination of this table reveals that most of the strategic challenges faced by organizations are, in fact, environmental challenges. He then developed a simple conceptual scheme for the strategic challenge-response process and hypothesized the following:

(1) That alterations in a firm's strategy set (objectives, strategy, functional policies) result from either actual or forecast changes in its external environment and/or in its resources and capabilities . . . ; (2) that different types of strategic challenges would elicit different strategic responses; and (3) that the type of strategic response adopted for a specific strategic challenge would, in general, significantly influence the future success or failure of the firm. [P. 47]

TABLE 2.7

The Perceptually Based Strategy Model

Perceived Environmental Uncertainty	Perceived Need for Internal Change			
	Code	Low	Code	High
Certain		Cell 1		Cell 2
	1	Fixed and well defined	1	Need for identification and readjustment
	2	Optimization; maintenance; efficiency	2	Optimization; improve economies of operation; planned change
	3	Process planning; maintain competence	3	Process planning; integration; improve distinctive competence
	4	Closed-stable-mechanistic	4	Closed-stable-mechanistic
	5	Commitment to existing power structure; less active search for environmental information	5	Commitment to existing power structure; systematic; conservative; less active search for environmental information; "integrative," entrepreneur
Uncertain		Cell 3		Cell 4
	1	Continually adjusted to feedback	1	Varied and flexible
	2	Satisficing; maintain capacity to cope with uncertainty	2	Satisficing; survival; develop effective problem solving
	3	Adaptive or contingency planning; search of advance information; penetration	3	Adaptive or contingency planning; divestiture; merger diversification
	4	Open-adaptive-organic	4	Open-adaptive-organic
	5	Adaptive planner; information gathering	5	Search for external information; adaptive; "sharp departure" entrepreneur

1 = mission or domain
2 = objectives
3 = strategies and policies
4 = organization form
5 = role performance of policy maker

Source: Carl R. Anderson and Frank T. Paine, "Managerial Perceptions and Strategic Behavior," Academy of Management Journal 18 (1975): 817.

The result of Hofer's preliminary study indicated "that different types of strategic challenges do indeed elicit different types of strategic responses" (p. 51).

Since the strategy formulation process is considered to be a crucial part of organization-environment interaction, Anderson and Paine (1975) have developed a perceptually based strategy model (see Table 2.7) to provide some insights into the environment/strategy-formulation/internal-properties interaction. The model is based on two perceptual variables: environmental uncertainty and the need for internal change.

> In order to enhance understanding, each perceptual variable has been reduced to two dimensions: perceptions of environmental certainty and uncertainty, and low and high perceived need for change. The resulting four quadrants present different kinds of strategy formulation problems which require different strategies for effective solution. The model is intended as a framework for analysis of the strategy formulation process. [P. 816]

In a discussion of strategic moves in each of the four quadrants, Anderson and Paine note that

> while there is (depending on the stage of development, share of market, and forecasted market growth rate) an opportunity to exercise a great deal of discretion in each quadrant, each of the four quadrants seems to be associated with a set of possible strategic moves (or outputs) for the organization or division, based on the appropriate perceptions. [P. 819]

Khandwalla (1976) views an organization's strategy as a response to its environment. His study of 79 firms generally confirmed that a comprehensive or multifaceted strategy denotes a dynamic, complex, and uncertain environment.

Segal (1974, p. 212) indicates that "organizational response to its environment" is related to the organization's internal structure (interrelationship and overall management of units). It is also related to the organization's decision-making process (basis of decision and assessment) and its boundary-spanning strategy (basis of support and extent of decentralization).

Salancik, Pfeffer, and Kelly (1974) discussed the source of influence in organizational decision making and argued that

> influence derives from an individual's ability to reduce organizational uncertainty and that, when the nature of

this uncertainty varies across organization decision contexts, the characteristics associated with this capability are also likely to vary. . . . Influence determination works through a communication process which serves to define the source of uncertainty and to locate individuals capable of coping with the uncertainty. [P. 55]

Hickson, Hinings, Lee, Schneck, and Pennings (1971) propose a strategic contingencies theory of intraorganizational power that seems relevant to our concepts of environmental uncertainty and relative importance of different organizational functions. Modern organizations have to cope with environmentally derived uncertainties in the sources and composition of inputs, the processing of throughputs, and the disposal of outputs in order to ensure adequate task performance. Hickson, Hinings, Lee, Schneck, and Pennings (1971) related coping with uncertainty by a subunit to its power and offered the following hypothesis: "The more a subunit copes with uncertainty, the greater its power within the organization" (p. 220). However, in terms of this study, this hypothesis can be restated as follows: When uncertainty facing a functional unit is very high, then the more the functional unit copes with uncertainty, the greater is its strategic significance within the organization. Thus, the subunit that enjoys the greatest power in the organization is not necessarily the one facing the most uncertainty but the one that copes most effectively with the most uncertainty. The source of power, therefore, lies not in the high level of uncertainty per se, but in the subunit's ability to cope effectively with high uncertainty. Such a subunit acts as a "shock absorber" for the whole organization; it diminishes the impact of uncertainty on other subunits, which tend to see themselves as more and more dependent on that subunit. Thus, the perceived effectiveness of a subunit in coping with a high level of uncertainty and the increased number and degree of dependencies created by such coping behavior result in that subunit acquiring more and more power within the organization.

Bobbitt, Randolph, and Ford (1980) note that "when the decision environment is perceived as uncertain decision makers may deal with the uncertainty by changing their perceptions through avoidance, delay, reduction, or absorption" (p. 23). Decision makers may attempt to cope with uncertainty through modeling, or by reducing it through alternative generalization, or by acquiring more information, or by changing the consequences. In the latter case, they may attempt to transfer the location of uncertainty through contracting or to reduce it through proactive strategies. Finally, they cope with uncertainty by maintaining a highly flexible and responsive structure. When the environment is perceived as one of complexity (that is, large, heterogeneous, abstract, or highly interconnected and interrelated), it may be modeled through such strategies as decomposition.

Miles and Snow (1978) examined the relationship between the managerial perceptions of environmental uncertainty and the relative strategic importance of different organizational functions.

> The findings of this study suggest some support that when the organization faces high environmental uncertainty, it places greater emphasis on externally oriented functions such as market research and product development. Conversely, when an organization faces low uncertainty, internally oriented functions (such as production) assume strategic importance. [P. 213]

Hambrick and Snow (1977), in consideration of Thompson's (1967) work, suggest that

> in order to understand fully why a particular strategic alternative is chosen also requires knowledge of the environmental and organizational context in which the decision is made. . . . Because of their importance, strategic decisions must be closely linked with each other to form a consistent pattern. This pattern is called strategy, an ongoing stream of decisions aimed at effectively "matching" or aligning organizational resources with environmental opportunities and constraints. [P. 109]

Their contextual model of strategic decision making is shown in Figure 2.3. Hambrick and Snow believe that the role of managerial perceptions of environmental and organizational variables in the strategic decision-making process is extremely important and that a useful conceptualization of this role requires a sequential view of the perceptual process. In the first place, a manager's field of vision cannot and does not encompass every aspect of the organization and its environment. Thus, a manager's perceptions are primarily determined by (or limited to) those areas comprising his field of vision. Therefore, his perceptions are also limited to those areas within his field of vision selectively perceived by him. Finally, a manager's age, his functional orientation, his position in the managerial echelon, and his value system collectively constitute a filter through which the mass of information to be processed by him is interpreted. According to Hambrick and Snow,

> This field of vision-selective perception-interpretation sequence for considering the conversion of information

FIGURE 2.3

A Contextual Model of Strategic Decision Making

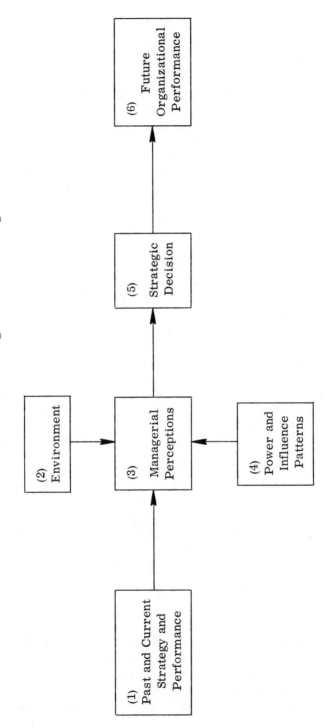

Source: Donald C. Hambrick and Charles C. Snow, "A Contextual Model of Strategic Decision Making in Organizations," Academy of Management Proceedings, 1977, p. 110. Reprinted by permission of Donald C. Hambrick, Columbia University, and Charles C. Snow, The Pennsylvania State University.

35

into a set of managerial perceptions that subsequently guides decision making appears to be useful in organizing the relevant literature. [1977, p. 110; emphasis added]

Duncan (1972) also suggests that the environmental characteristics are "dependent on the perception of organizational members and thus can vary in their incidence to the extent that individuals differ in their perceptions" (p. 325).

Weed and Mitchell (1980) comment that uncertainty about the surrounding environment is described as unpleasant and detrimental to effective decision making and performance. A structured task results in less environmental uncertainty than does an unstructured one. Higher environmental uncertainty is related to more errors and lower accuracy and satisfaction.

According to Starbuck (1976), organizations select those aspects of the environment with which they would deal based on their perceptions of the environment. Thus, the organizational strategies to deal with the environment are based on the process of selection and perception of environment. This is similar to Weick's (1969, 1977) contention that organizations do not merely respond to their external environments; they, in fact, "enact" or shape their own environments through a series of strategic decisions over a period of time.

The recognizable pattern of an organization's responses to environmental issues (Child 1972a; Miles, Snow, and Pfeffer 1974; Richards 1973) is determined not so much by the objective characteristics of organization-environment interactions as by the managerial perceptions of the environmental conditions. This study's approach is based on the managerial perceptions of the strategic significance of key result areas in different organizational functions.

Corporate strategy and critical environments are believed to be related. A firm can benefit from an understanding of the nature of its strategic or critical environments in the process of formulating its corporate strategy. It has been demonstrated that the functional strategies (as a component of corporate strategy) can and do reflect the perceived conditions of the firm's strategic environments (Godiwalla, Meinhart, and Warde 1979).

Bourgeois (1980) notes that an important responsibility of management is the formulation of corporate strategies to guide organizational activities, and that such guidance may be accomplished through appropriate coalignment of organizational resources with environmental segments. In order for the firm to continue to thrive, it must conceive and achieve appropriate alignment with its environment. In this regard, many business-policy scholars believe that corporate strategy is the mechanism through which proper alignment is achieved.

Various authors (Emery and Trist, Thompson, Burns and Stalker, Lawrence and Lorsch, Duncan, and Downey et al.) have tried to describe and measure the environment in a manner that is conceptually and analytically useful. Generally, the attention is focused on change as an important dimension. However, some authors have not recognized the distinction between the rate of environmental change and the degree of environmental uncertainty or the unpredictability of change. Where an organization is faced with rapid but mostly predictable change in the environment, it is not really faced with environmental uncertainty; it can predict reasonably well the kind of environmental conditions it will have to face in the future. This study will utilize Miles and Snow's (1978) framework for determining the managerial perceptions of environmental uncertainty, in which the behavior of the various subenvironments will be rated on the degree of their predictability or certainty.

Technology

The primary production system employed by the organization significantly affects the strategic, structural, and scale (size) aspects of the organization. It also affects the strategic mix of organizational functions through its impact on the degree of labor intensity, capital intensity (and therefore automation), knowledge intensity (and therefore research), and energy intensity. Woodward (1965) suggests that a relationship exists between the organization's technology and its control system, and therefore structural dimensions of an organization might be related to the level of its technical achievement.

Perrow (1970) has classified organizations into four technology types based on the analyzability of the search process and the number and frequency of exceptions to normal problem-solving processes. These four technology types are craft, nonroutine, routine, and engineering. Perrow contends that problems faced by each organization are different, and therefore the technological and structural requirements of each are also different.

The predominant production system used in the organization determines the nature of its technological subenvironment and the pattern of the organization's responses to that subenvironment. For instance, in the Lawrence and Lorsch (1967) study, the findings indicated that

> special organizational divisions were established (research and development) to keep the organization current; in other organizations, departments such as industrial engineering, management analysis, and so on, are so designated. [Hall 1977, p. 304]

FIGURE 2.4

Classification of Work-Unit Technologies

Task
Knowledge

Not Well Understood	Craft	Research
Well Understood	Programmable	Technical-Professional

Low   Task   High

Source: Richard L. Daft and Norman B. McIntosh, "A New Approach to Design and Use of Management Information." Copyright 1978 by the Regents of the University of California. Reprinted from California Management Review, vol. 21, no. 1, p. 85, by permission of the Regents.

Thompson (1967) developed a series of propositions about organizations with technology as a major determinant of structure. He examined the interrelationships between technology and other variables, such as size, environment, and structure. He classified technology into three basic groups: mediating, intensive, and long-linked. The efforts needed to coordinate and control the organization's "technical core" are different for each, and therefore the technology employed significantly impacts the structural dimensions and processes.

Murphy (1972) investigated the effects of technology on organizational decentralization and concluded that the change and complexity arising from the adoption of new technological processes have a direct and specific impact on decentralization in the organization. His findings suggest

that other things being equal: (1) firms with a more complex technological process tend to be more decentralized than firms with a less complex technological process, and (2) firms with a more dynamic technological process tend to be more decentralized than firms with a less dynamic technological process. [P. 65]

Hickson, Pugh, and Pheysey (1969) in their study of work organization in Birmingham, England, found no support for the sweeping "technological imperative" hypothesis that technology and structure are strongly related. However, the technology-structure relationship was more profound and pervasive in small organizations. In large organizations, operations technology was shown to affect only those variables related to the workflow rather than the broader administrative and hierarchical aspects of structure.

Daft and McIntosh (1978) developed a technology grid based on Perrow's work by combining two dimensions of technology: task knowledge (known ways of responding to problems) and task variety (frequency of unexpected and novel problems). The grid then forms the basis for classifying work-unit technology into four categories: programmable, technical-professional, research, and craft (see Figure 2.4).

Woodward's classification scheme was chosen for this study because it is the least abstract and best suited to this study's design.

Size and Structure

Size of the organization also has an important influence on the various strategic and structural variables. It dictates an organization's strategic postures and affects such variables as complexity, span of control of senior executives, management levels, and the size of the administrative component. Size may be a function of age, organization's past strategies and performance, and the stage at which the organization finds itself in the organizational life cycle. Size is also interrelated with the industry structure (Burack 1975) and the predominant production system used in the organization. However, most of the empirical work in the area of organizational size relates to its impact on organizational structure. The research findings suggest that size cannot be considered as the major determinant of structure. Other variables must be taken into account for understanding organizational structure.

The Aston Group[1] found technology to be of much less importance than size to organization structure. However, Aldrich (1972) reanalyzed the Aston Group findings using path analysis, and technology emerged as a variable of major importance.

In a survey article on the role of size as a variable in studies of organization structure, Kimberly (1976) argues "that size has generally been defined in terms too global to permit its relation to organizational structure to be understood adequately" (p. 571). He advocates the need for a more differentiated view of size, so that researchers can study differential relationships between different aspects of size and different dimensions of structure.

> A more flexible view in which at certain times and under certain conditions certain aspects of size may be conceptualized as dimensions of context seems preferable. The question of causality, of the causal connection between size and structure, becomes similarly redefined. No longer does it make sense to ask whether size causes structure or structure causes size, but rather under what conditions aspects of size are determinants of dimensions of structure, under what conditions the two covary, and under what conditions dimensions of structure are determinants of aspects of size. [P. 594]

Pugh, Hickson, Hinings, and Turner (1969) analyzed the relationships between the structure of an organization and the context in which it functions. Using contextual variables as independent variables in a multivariate prediction analysis of the structural factors, the researchers found size to be the first predictor ($r = 0.69$) of structuring of activities; however, with work-flow integration (a technological dimension) added as a predictor, the multiple correlation increased to 0.75. The researchers concluded that

> the size of the correlations inevitably raise the question of causal implications. It is tempting to argue that these clear relationships are causal in particular, that size, dependence, and the charter-technology-location nexus largely determine structure. [P. 112]

Child (1975) investigated the nature of influence of company performance and environmental variability on the rate of development in organization structure as company size increases. He found that the different categories of companies could be arranged in a sequence, as presented in Figure 2.5.

Child (1975) further observed the following:

> The relative order of high performers in variable and stable environments suggests that environmental contingencies may interact with scale contingencies. . . . It appears, then, that management has to pay regard to multiple contingencies, such as those of environment

FIGURE 2.5

Company Performance, Organization Structure, and Size

Rate of Development in
Organization Structure
as Company Size Increases

Low

1. Below-average performers in
   stable environments
2. Below-average performers in
   variable environments
3. Above-average performers in
   variable environments
4. Above-average performers in
   stable environments

High

Source: John Child, "Managerial and Organizational Factors
Associated with Company Performance—Part II. A Contingency
Analysis," Journal of Management Studies 12 (1975): 22.

and scale together, when planning the design of its organization. [Pp. 22-24]

Child (1970), in relating the concepts of structuring of activities
and decentralization with strategies of administrative control, offers
an alternative interpretation of the Aston Group's[2] findings.

Within certain limits imposed by the organization's operating situation, managers appear to have a choice between:
(a) maintaining control directly by confining decisions to
fairly senior levels. This economizes on the need for
systems of procedures and paperwork and reduces the
overhead of indirect specialized personnel to operate and
maintain the systems, or (b) maintaining control indirectly
by relying on the use of procedures, paper records, and
on the employment of expert specialists to make decisions
at lower levels (within the limits of discretion imposed by
the indirect controls). [P. 378]

Theoretical Synthesis of the Concepts of Size,
Technology, Environment, and Structure

In a review of literature pertaining to the influence of three contingency variables—size, technology, and environment—on different
dimensions of organization structure, Ford and Slocum (1977) summarize the relationship between structure and contingency variables
(see Table 2.8). As is evident from Table 2.8, each of the three contingency variables can offer similar predictions of structural dimensions. It is, therefore, possible that relationships observed in studies
that considered only one contingency variable might be attributable
to one (or two) of the contingency variables not considered by the researcher. Since few studies considered all three contingency variables
simultaneously, the patterns of contingency-structure causality are
far from clear. Aside from the issue of effect independence, there
is also a high degree of interrelationships between technology, size,
and environmental uncertainty. The researcher must, therefore,
consider the interrelationships and their impact on the contingency-
structure relationships. Aside from this problem of independence,

TABLE 2.8

Summary of Contingency-Structure Relationships

	Technology (task routineness)	Size (number of members)	Environment (perceived uncertainty)
Administrative intensity	+	−	+
Complexity			
Horizontal	+	+	+
Vertical	+	+	
Spatial		+	
Personal	−		
Formalization	+	+	−
Centralization	+	−	−

Source: Jeffrey D. Ford and John W. Slocum, Jr., "Size,
Technology, Environment and the Structure of Organizations,"
Academy of Management Review 2 (1977): 571.

TABLE 2.9

A Theoretical Synthesis of the Concepts of Organizational Size, Technology, Complexity, and Structural Differentiation

Independent Variable	Dependent Variable	Theory
Level of task scope	Level of complexity	Positively related because the greater the number of clients and depth of involvement with them or the greater the variety of products and the difficulty of producing them, the greater the number of technologies and thus different occupational specialties because of the limits of cognition
Rate of task scope change	Rate of complexity change	Positively related because the addition of new clients or products requires new technologies, which in turn require new occupational specialties
Level of size	Level of complexity	Positively related only because large organizations achieve economies of scale that result in advantages in hiring occupational specialties in administrative areas
Rate of size change	Rate of complexity change	No relationship because the hiring of new personnel does not necessarily mean the hiring of new occupational specialties
Level of task scope	Level of vertical differentiation	Small positive relationship because technological complexity decreases spans and necessitates more levels
Rate of task scope change	Rate of vertical differentiation change	No relationship because new technologies are usually added horizontally, not vertically
Level of size	Level of vertical differentiation	Positively related because large numbers require many supervisors; there is a limit to the span of control
Rate of size change	Rate of vertical differentiation change	Small positive relationship because the hiring of new people, unless there are a large number of them, does not stress spans sufficiently to necessitate addition of new levels
Level of task scope	Level of horizontal differentiation	Positively related because different clients or products and/or technologies are usually housed in different departments for social and ecological reasons
Rate of task scope change	Rate of horizontal differentiation change	Positively related because new clients or products and/or technologies are usually housed in new departments
Level of size	Level of horizontal differentiation	Small positive relationship because of economies of scale that permit the hiring of ancillary specialists that are located in new departments
Rate of size change	Rate of horizontal differentiation change	No relationship because the addition of new people has no necessary relationship with the addition of departments

Source: Robert Dewar and Jerald Hage, "Size, Technology and Structural Differentiation: Toward a Theoretical Synthesis," Administrative Science Quarterly 23 (1978): 115.

Ford and Slocum identified two other problems in previous research. First, all the variables involved (technology, size, environment, and structure) have serious measurement problems; and second, units and levels of analysis are different in different research studies. Ford and Slocum conclude their review with the following remarks:

> Additional research might be directed toward better un-
> derstanding the relationship between contingency vari-
> ables and structure, and toward understanding the inter-
> relationships among the contingency variables themselves.
> That these variables are significantly interrelated and
> appear to influence each other's relationship to structure
> indicates that the current "single variable" approach may
> be misleading. [P. 572]

Dewar and Hage (1978) contend that "the relationships among size, complexity, technology, and structural differentiation are more complex than has been previously thought" (p. 132). They offer theoretical arguments (summarized in Table 2.9) relating levels and rates of technology and size to complexity and structural differentiation. Their findings suggest that task scope (a technological dimension) and not organizational size is the most important determinant of differentiation in the division of labor. Dewar and Hage conclude that

> by examining associations of levels and change rates it is
> possible to better understand how growth and increase in
> task scope affect both the complexity of the division of
> labor and structural differentiation. . . . Their indicators
> are different; the causal arguments are different; and the
> relative importance of size and technology as causal forces
> are different. Thus, we need to develop theories for each
> of these processes. They cannot, at least at this point,
> be theoretically synthesized. [P. 129]

Strategy and Structure

The importance of organization structure in strategic planning emanates primarily from the fact that strategic planning is essentially an organizationwide activity rather than something done merely by the planning department staff. Cleland and King (1974) so rightly point out the following:

> Strategic planning is a job to be performed by managers—
> not for them. However critical the role of professional

planning staff is to an effective strategic planning process, professional planners are not the doers of planning . . .; rather, they are the facilitators. The doers of strategic planning are managers—both top managers and lower-level line managers—thereby ensuring that the people who will be charged with implementing the plans are those who have generated the goals and developed and approved the plans. [P. 26]

In order to ensure successful implementation of strategies, Koontz (1976) highlights the need for making organization structure fit planning needs: "The organization structure should be designed to support the accomplishment of goals and the making of decisions to implement strategies" (p. 47).

Based on Chandler's (1962) pioneering study of strategy and structure, many researchers, notably from Harvard Business School, have attempted to examine the interrelationship between diversification strategy (similar to corporate diversity in this study) and organizational structure. Chandler showed how different strategies posed different degrees of administrative complexity and, therefore, tended to require different types of organizational structure. Rumelt (1974) found "that data gave strong support to Chandler's proposition that 'structure follows strategy' but forced the addition of 'structure also follows fashion'" (p. 149). According to Galbraith and Nathanson (1978),

Three main principles can be identified in Chandler's work: (1) Organization structure follows the growth strategy pursued by the firm; (2) American firms have followed a pattern of stagewise development from unifunctional structure, to the functional organization, to the multi-divisional structure; (3) The change from one stage to another occurred only after provocation, because the strategy formulator and organizational innovator were different types of people. [P. 16]

When a strategy-structure fit is disturbed in any organization, its performance tends to decline. However, Galbraith and Nathanson introduced competition as a mediating variable in the relationship between strategy and structure and thus modified Chandler's proposition. They stated that "only under competitive conditions does a mismatch between strategy and structure lead to ineffective performance" (1978, p. 139).

Fouraker and Stopford (1968) found that the organizations pursuing multinational growth strategy tend to have highly diversified

FIGURE 2.6

A Model of Organizational Adaptation to Mass Output Technology

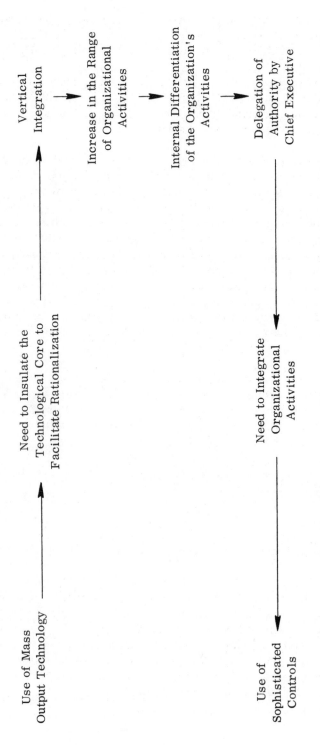

Source: Reprinted from Pradip N. Khandwalla, "Mass Output Orientation of Operations Technology and Organizational Structure," Administrative Science Quarterly 19 (1974): 79, by permission of the author and the publisher. Copyright © 1974 by the Administrative Science Quarterly.

domestic business with a proved R&D leadership; decentralized, divisionalized structure; and the ability to produce international general managers capable of controlling and guiding a highly diversified organization.

Khandwalla (1974) developed a model of organizational adaptation to mass output technology (see Figure 2.6), which was supported by data for 79 manufacturing firms. According to Khandwalla, the causal arrow in the model should be viewed

> as going from technology to vertical integration to organizational differentiation and decentralization of authority to the use of sophisticated controls as a powerful integrative and coordinating device. . . . The model incorporates three basic hypotheses for manufacturing organizations: (1) the more mass-output oriented the technology used by an organization, the more vertically integrated it is likely to be, (2) the more vertically integrated the organization is, the more decentralized is its top-level decision making likely to be, and (3) the more decentralized the top-level decision making, the more the organization is likely to use sophisticated controls to coordinate the activities of the organization. [P. 79]

Therefore, Khandwalla's (1974) study established a special form of technology-strategy-structure relationships, where the use of mass-output technology leads to the pursuit of vertical integration (a growth strategy), which in turn requires certain changes in the organizational structure and decision making. Such relationships were found to be more pronounced for high-profit firms.

In his study of corporate technological staff size in 21 large diversified firms, Pitts (1977) found systematic structural differences between firms pursuing two different diversification strategies—internal diversification and acquisitive diversification (in terms of this study, internal growth strategy and external acquisitive growth strategy, respectively). These differences are depicted schematically in Figure 2.7.

Miller and Springate (1978), in a study of functionally and divisionally organized firms in the retailing industry, found that in product-divisional organizational structures, comparable decisions tend to be made at lower levels of the organization than in functional organizational structures. As regards performance measurement and control systems, product-divisional organizations were found to rely more on predetermined and clearly specified norms of performance. Miller and Springate conclude that

FIGURE 2.7

Structural Differences in Firms Pursuing Different Diversification Strategies

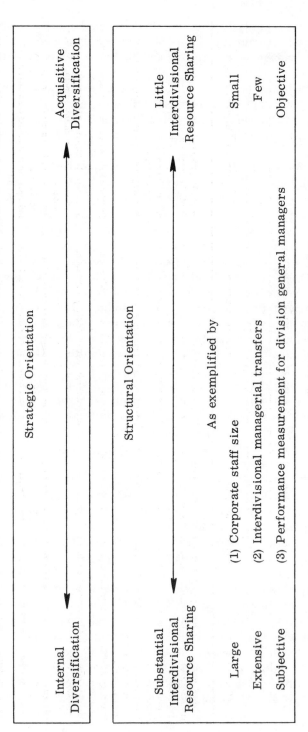

Source: Reprinted from Robert A. Pitts, "Strategies and Structures for Diversification," Academy of Management Journal 20 (1977): 199, by permission of the author and the publisher. Copyright © 1977 by the Academy of Management Journal.

TABLE 2.10

Corporate Life Cycle: Three Stages and Company Characteristics

Company Characteristics	Stage		
	1 (or small company)	2 (or integrated company)	3 (or diversified company)
Product line	Single product or single-product line	Single-product line	Multiple-product lines
Distribution pipeline	One channel or set of channels	One set of channels	Multiple channels
Organization structure	Little formal structure; one-man show	Specialization based on functional areas	Specialization based on market-product relationships
Intracompany product/service transactions	No pattern of intracompany transactions	Integrated intracompany transactions	Nonintegrated, pattern of transactions
R&D organization process	Not institutionalized; guided by owner-manager	Institutionalized search of product or process improvements	Institutionalized search for new products as well as for improvements
Performance measurements	By personal contact and subjective criteria	Increasingly impersonal, using technical/cost criteria	Increasingly impersonal, using market criteria (return on investment, market share)
Rewards	Unsystematic and often paternalistic	Systematic with emphasis on stability and service	Systematic with variability related to performance
Control system	Personal control of strategic decisions	Personal control of strategic decisions	Indirect control based on analysis of "results"
Operating decisions	Personal control of operating decisions	Increasing delegation of operating decisions through policy	Delegation of market-product decisions within existing businesses
Strategic choices	Needs of owner versus needs of company	Degree of integration, market share objective; breadth of product line	Entry and exit from industries; allocation of resources by industry; rate of growth

Source: Roman V. Tuason, Jr., "Corporate Life Cycle and the Evaluation of Corporate Strategy," Academy of Management Proceedings (1973), p. 37. Adapted from B. R. Scott, "The Industrial State: Old Myths and New Realities," Harvard Business Review 51 (March-April 1973): 133-48.

TABLE 2.11

Cannon's Stages of Development

Characteristic	Stage				
	1 Entrepreneurial	2 Functional Development	3 Decentralization	4 Staff Proliferation	5 Recentralization
Strategic decisions	Made mostly by top man	Made more and more by other managers	May have "loss of control"	Corporate staff assists in decisions	Corporate management makes the decisions
Organization structure	Informal operations	Specialization based on functions	To cope with problems of functionalization; By industry or product division	Corporate staff assists the chief executive	Similar to stage 2
Communication and climate	From leader down; informal communication	Internal communication is important and difficult		Conservatism may result in slower communications	
Control system	Minimal need for coordination and control	Concerned with everyday situations	Problems with control	May be problems between line and staff	Tightening of control

Source: William F. Glueck, Business Policy: Strategy Formation and Management Action (New York: McGraw-Hill, 1976), p. 237.

TABLE 2.12

Key Factors in Top Management Process in Stage 1, 2, and 3 Companies

Key Factors in Management Process	Stage 1	Stage 2	Stage 3
Size up major problems	Survival and growth, dealing with short-term operating problems	Growth, rationalization, and expansion of resources, providing for adequate attention to product problems	Trusteeship in management and investment control of large, increasing, and diversified resources. Also, important to diagnose and take action on problems at division level
Objectives	Personal and subjective	Profits and meeting functionally oriented budgets and performance targets	ROI, profits, earnings per share
Strategy	Implicit and personal, exploitation of immediate opportunities seen by owner-manager	Functionally oriented moves restricted to "one product" scope, exploitation of one basic product or service field	Growth and product diversification, exploitation of general business opportunities
Organization: major characteristic of structure	One unit "one man show"	One unit functionally specialized group	Multiunit general staff office and decentralized operating divisions
Measurement and control	Personal, subjective, control based on simple accounting system and daily communication and observation	Control grows beyond one man, assessment of functional operations necessary, structured control systems evolve	Complex formal system geared to comparative assessment of performance measures, indicating problems and opportunities and assessing management ability of division managers
Key performance indicators	Personal criteria, relationships with owner, operating efficiency, ability to solve operating problems	Functional and internal criteria such as sales, performance compared with budget, size of empire, status in group, personal relationships, and the like	More impersonal application of comparisons such as profits, ROI, P/E ratio, sales, market share, productivity, product leadership, personnel development, employee attitudes, public responsibility
Reward-punishment system	Informal, personal, subjective, used to maintain control and divide small pool of resources to provide personal incentives for key performers	More structured, usually based to a greater extent on agreed policies as opposed to personal opinion and relationships	Allotment by "due process" of a wide variety of different rewards and punishments on a formal and systematic basis. Companywide policies usually apply to many different classes of managers and workers with few major exceptions for individual cases

Source: Donald H. Thain, "Stages of Corporate Development," Business Quarterly 34 (Winter 1969): 42.

in essence, the general pattern established has been that
product divisionals operate with a markedly different set
of management, process and decision making especially
as regards the "autonomy" of certain management roles,
particularly at lower levels in the organization. [P. 125]

Out of Chandler's (1962) research, a group of theorists called
"stages of growth and development theorists" have developed different
stages of growth models. These models go beyond a mere examination of strategy-structure relationships and develop a concept of a
corporate life cycle with distinct stages of corporate development.

On the basis of the Scott model (1973), Tuason (1973) has identified three stages of a corporate life cycle, each stage having different company characteristics (see Table 2.10).

Glueck (1976) has summarized Cannon's (1968) theory of five
stages of development in the form of a table (see Table 2.11). Glueck
observes the following:

Cannon does not contend that companies move through these
stages in sequence, or that they move through all the stages.
It is not clear how and why firms decentralize or why they
go through these stages. What Cannon does say is that if
the firm is in Stage [2], the organizational characteristic
of specialization by function is present. [P. 237]

Thain (1969) has identified three main stages of corporate development (see Table 2.12). Stage 1 companies are generally simple
and small, whereas Stage 3 companies are large and complex. Thain
concedes that not all companies can be classified in any one of the
stages, since many companies would be in a phase of transition from
Stage 1 to Stage 2 or from Stage 2 to Stage 3.

Smith and Charmoz (1975) provide a good example of a growth
and development model for a multinational corporation. Figure 2.8
illustrates their five-phase model of the evolution of control, coordination, and organizational crises in the development of multinational corporations (Galbraith and Nathanson 1978, pp. 107-10).

Galbraith and Nathanson (1978) offer their own considerably re-
fined model of corporate growth and development (see Figure 2.9).
It essentially summarizes the main concepts of the earlier models
and builds on the available empirical evidence. The stages of growth
in this model are neither discrete nor sequential thereby permitting
alternate paths through the developmental sequence. Besides, the
model also empirically illustrates the dominant (not universal) growth
path taken by U.S. firms.

Quinn (1980) argues that many executives would be more happy
over the quality of implementation of strategies if they utilize logical

FIGURE 2.8

Evolution of Control, Coordination, and Organizational Crises in the Development of a Multinational Corporation

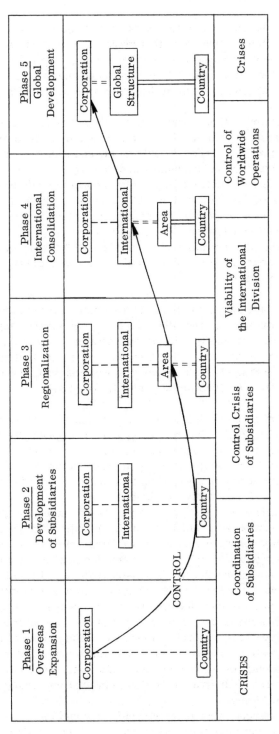

Coordination Patterns:

- - - - represents mutual adjustment (coordination by checking only as problems arise)

= = = = represents planning (coordination through tops-down planning)

——— represents policy and procedure (coordination through establishment of policies and procedures)

Source: William Smith and R. Charmoz, "Coordinate Line Management" (Working Paper, Searle International, Chicago, February 1975). Reproduced by permission of Searle International.

FIGURE 2.9

A Summary of Stages Model

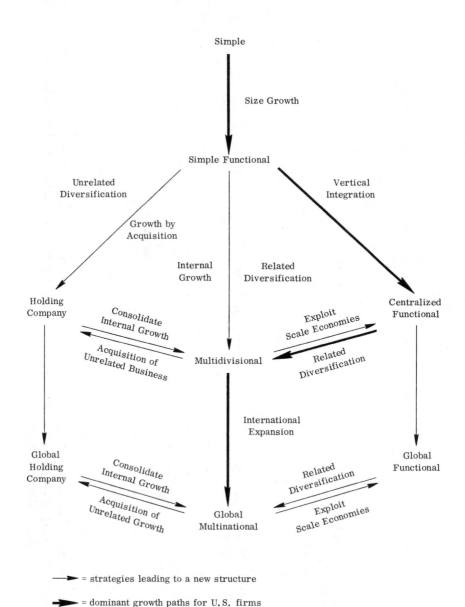

Source: Reprinted by permission from Jay R. Galbraith and Daniel A. Nathanson, Strategy Implementation: The Role of Structure and Process (St. Paul: West, 1978), p. 115. Copyright © 1978 by West Publishing Company. All rights reserved.

54

FIGURE 2.10

The Role of Organizational Slack and the Contingent Nature of Strategy and Structure

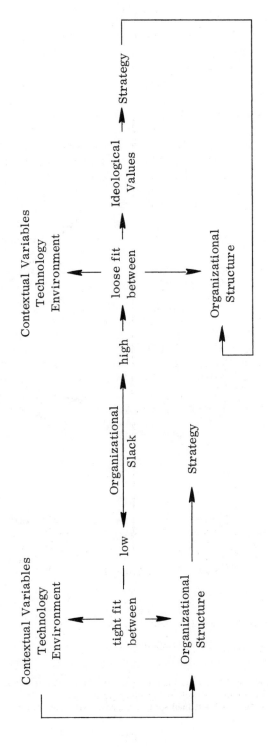

Source: Reprinted from Robert J. Litschert and T. W. Bonham, "A Conceptual Model of Strategy Formation," Academy of Management Review 3 (1978): 216, by permission of the author and the publisher. Copyright © 1978 by the Academy of Management Review.

and incremental action for improving the quality of information generated and the implementation process. Formulation and implementation should not be viewed as distinct processes but, rather, as parts of the same overall framework. Improved organizational awareness and psychological commitment to strategies are vital to the effective implementation.

Based on the empirical research of and theoretical models developed by organization theorists as business-policy researchers, Litschert and Bonham (1978) developed a conceptual model of strategy formation (see Figure 2.10) where organizational slack[3] is a crucial moderator variable influencing the necessary fit between structure and contextual variables (technology and environment) and ultimately the causal direction of the strategy-structure relationship. Thus, the level of organizational slack is a major determinant of the contingent nature of strategy. The authors contend that

> slack affects the direction of the strategy-structure relationship by influencing the necessary fit between organization structure and the interactive effects of technologies and environments. When slack is low, there are no excess resources to pay the price of a structural design different from that dictated by the interactive effects of these contextual variables. Necessary fit is tight, and strategy is determined by structure, at least in part. When slack is relatively high, excess resources are available to pay the price of a structural design which may stray from the contingent requirements of contextual variables. In this case, necessary fit may be loose because economic sacrifice is minimized, and strategy is likely to be more contingent on the ideological values of the dominant coalition. [P. 217]

The contingency theory of organizational structure states that there is no one best way to organize, nor are all ways of organizing equally effective. Organizational theorists (notably Burns and Stalker, and Lawrence and Lorsch) consider the rate of change in the environment as a determinant of the organizational form. This point of view is consistent with Chandler's strategy-structure hypothesis, since organizations, rather than responding to their given external environments, "enact" (Weick 1969, 1977) or shape their own environments through a series of strategic decisions over a period of time. A high degree of corporate diversity (itself the result of past strategies and performance) means that the organization is simultaneously operating in many different product-market domains. As Khandwalla (1977) points out, "Typically but not exclusively, diversified organizations

FIGURE 2.11

Contingency Paradigm

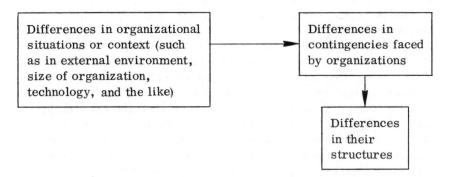

Source: Pradip N. Khandwalla, The Design of Organizations (New York: Harcourt Brace Jovanovich, 1977), p. 236.

tend to have highly variegated environments" (p. 337). Thus, the rate and the predictability of the environmental changes are very often determined by the strategies pursued by the organization. As organizations grow in size and become more diverse through the adoption of certain strategies, more decentralized subunits are formed for effective strategy implementation. The extent of decentralization (which is an important characteristic of organizational structure) depends on the need for environmental adaptability. Therefore, it also depends on autonomy of differentiated subunits and the need for integration of those subunits. The contingency paradigm presented by Khandwalla (1977) is shown in Figure 2.11.

The relationships between corporate strategy and structural and administrative decisions (advocated by Chandler 1962 and others) and the relationships between a firm's structural and administrative decisions and its environmental complexity and uncertainty (advocated by organizational theorists like Burns and Stalker 1961; Lawrence and Lorsch 1967b; Woodward 1965; and others) are gradually evolving into a contingency theory of the firm that looks like the one charted by Ward (1976) in Table 2.13.

As Richards (1978) points out, the organizational structure is important in the formulation and implementation of strategy

> because the locus of planning, goal setting and decision-making is dependent upon the type of structure in which the planning is done. . . . The hierarchical nature of goals

TABLE 2.13

A Contingency Theory of the Firm

Organizational Administration	=	f(Strategic Choice)	=	f(Environment and Corporate Resources)
Structure		Product markets		Uncertainty
Organizational decision making process and climate		Competitive advantage		Human needs
Resource allocation		Goals and objectives		Life-cycle stage of industry's products
Reward systems		Policies and actions		Production technology
				Market dominance

Source: John L. Ward, "The Opportunity to Measure Strategic Variables: An Attempt to Quantify Product-Market Diversity," Journal of Economics and Business 28 (Spring-Summer 1976): 219.

and subgoals stems from organizational hierarchy. Much of the planning that is performed at the product division level in the larger diversified organizations is performed at the corporate level in single product functionally organized organizations (Galbraith and Nathanson, 1978). Additionally, there is a correspondence between the hierarchy of organization structure and the hierarchy of strategies. [P. 25]

Therefore, in corporate strategy research the interactions between size, diversity, and structure assume considerable importance.

CONCLUSION

The purpose of this chapter has been to survey the relevant literature from business-policy and organization theory to provide a proper theoretical base for the study. The theoretical and empirical literature, pertaining to the key concepts relevant to the development of this study's conceptual framework, has been broadly reviewed.

The definitions and operational measures of specific concepts directly relevant to this study's conceptual framework are explained in Chapter 3. Chapter 4 describes the study's conceptual framework and poses and discusses the research questions investigated by the study.

NOTES

1. Research on organization structure carried on by D. S. Pugh and his colleagues at the University of Aston in England.

2. Ibid.

3. Organizational slack is a hypothetical construct developed by the well-known troika of organization theorists, Cyert, March, and Simon. March and Simon (1958) define organizational slack as the "difference between the resources available to the organization and the total requirements of the members of the organizational coalition" (p. 126).

3

DEFINITIONS,
CONCEPTS, AND
MEASURES

INTRODUCTION

There are no generally accepted definitions or measures of most of the concepts constituting this study's conceptual framework. This has posed serious difficulties in operationalizing concepts to test them in real work settings, and the lack of clear-cut definitions and operational measures of research variables has been a major factor in the slow development of a coherent and unified body of theory of business policy. The data for this study were collected through mail questionnaires designed to be completed by senior corporate executives. It is, therefore, essential that the concepts and measurement techniques be formulated in a manner that would be managerially meaningful and that would accurately (and in the least possible time) capture the essence of top management's assertions and perceptions about various aspects of their firm's operations and environments. In view of the extreme pressure of time and the propensities of the working executives, questionnaires necessarily must be viable so that the response rate is satisfactory enough. This chapter explains the definitions and measures of eight key concepts underlying this study's conceptual framework as outlined in Figure 1.1.

GRAND CORPORATE STRATEGY

For the purpose of this study <u>grand corporate strategy</u> is defined as the major plan of action for achieving the sales and earnings goals for the company as a whole rather than a product, division, or market segment. The scope is the entire enterprise. In other words, the grand corporate strategy is the overall, primary, predominant, and single most important and vital master strategy of the firm. As Newman (1971, p. 20) points out, the "master strategy" refers to the entire pattern of company's basic mission, purposes, objectives, policies, and specific resource deployment (Steiner and Miner 1977, p. 20; emphasis added). Paine and Naumes (1974) define an overall or corporate strategy

> as a plan which encompasses not only the mission, policies, objectives and more specific goals of the organization, but also a plan of action for achieving these objectives and goals. . . . An overall strategy, then, is the sum total or pattern of . . . past and present actions or decisions. [P. 7]

Other well-known definitions of corporate strategy implicitly relate to grand corporate strategy discussed earlier because of their overall corporate orientation. Consider, for instance, definitions by Chandler and Glueck. Chandler (1962) defined strategy as "the determination of basic long-term goals and objectives of an enterprise, and the adoption of courses of action and the allocation of resources necessary for carrying out these goals" (p. 16). Glueck (1976) defines a strategy as "a unified comprehensive and integrated plan designed to assure that the basic objectives of the enterprise are achieved" (p. 3). Thus, the definition of grand corporate strategy used in this study is consistent with the definitions used by well-known authors in the field of business policy.

It should also be clear that the definition of grand corporate strategy is based on the overall nature of its scope. For this reason, such a strategy is formulated for and encompasses the activities of the company as a whole rather than a business, division, product, market, or functional area. Thus, a conglomerate will have many different business strategies, but will have only one grand corporate strategy that will encompass the entire enterprise. Similarly, a multidivisional company will have many different divisional strategies, but will still have only one grand corporate strategy for achieving the sales and earnings goals of the company as a whole. In fact, grand corporate strategy provides a groundwork from which different substrategies are derived.

The survey respondents (chief executive officers) were asked to identify their primary or single most important strategy as their grand corporate strategy from a normative classification of grand corporate strategies derived from Glueck (1976) and delineated in Appendix C (Chief Executive Officer's Questionnaire). The strategies were classified under four broad heads:

Stability strategies
Internal growth strategies
External acquisitive growth strategies
Retrenchment strategies

This normative list of strategies classifies the listed strategies for their purpose and function. Since the strategies follow corporate objectives (or more precisely, since strategies are plans of action to achieve specific corporate objectives), they are naturally purpose-oriented or functional (that is, they are meant to do certain things). Based on the respondents' identification, the subject firms were therefore classified into four categories of grand corporate strategies.

RELATIVE STRATEGIC SIGNIFICANCE OF DIFFERENT ORGANIZATIONAL FUNCTIONS

This study explores the nature of relationships between the grand corporate strategies pursued by industrial firms and top managers' perceptions of the relative importance (to effective strategy implementation) of different organizational functions. For this purpose the following seven organizational functions were identified:

1. General administration
2. Production/operations
3. Engineering and research and development
4. Marketing
5. Finance
6. Personnel
7. Public and government relations

However, the senior executives were not asked to merely rank these functions in order of importance or to evaluate each function in terms of its strategic significance on a Likert-type rating scale. A normative list of functionally grouped key result areas or strategic factors was first developed, and the senior executives were then asked to rate each key result area separately in terms of its strategic significance. Initially, a very detailed checklist of 99 key result areas relevant to industrial firms was prepared. This checklist is presented in Appendix A. However, it was readily apparent that to ensure adequate response from the participating firms, the list should be kept to a manageable length. Ultimately, the number of key result areas was reduced by almost 50 percent, and a revised normative list of functionally grouped key result areas (as shown in Appendix C—Senior Executive's Questionnaire) was used in the study.

When classified in this manner, the key result areas reflect the functional goals, strategies, policies, programs, roles, and structure. The key result areas have a significant impact upon organizational performance and, therefore, are critical to the firm's continued success. The key result areas are key organizational variables. They may also be called strategic factors, critical factors, key success factors, performance variables, pulse points, limiting factors (Anthony 1965, p. 139), and critical success factors (CSFs) (Rockart 1979).

According to Steiner,

> strategic factor refers to an action, element or condition which for a business may be of critical importance in its success or failure. It can refer both to a force outside the company as well as one within the enterprise. Success, as the word is used in this survey refers to the desired achievement of major objectives and goals established for your company. [1969a, p. 2]

A company's performance in its different key result areas should influence the effective implementation of its grand corporate strategy. However, the relative strategic significance of different key result areas would be different for companies having different grand corporate strategies. Therefore, top managers of different firms having different grand corporate strategies would perceive in different ways the relative strategic significance of key result areas in the various organizational functions.

Since each company is unique and has a distinct identity, it must determine its own key result areas in different organizational functions. However, a list of these key result areas common to all industrial companies (the subject of this study) can be prepared on the basis of past cumulative studies, research, and managerial experience. Key result areas listed in Appendix A and Appendix C are derived primarily from Steiner's (1969a) empirical study of strategic factors in business success and also from the works of the American Institute of Management (1961); Anthony and Dearden (1976); Buchele (1962); Glueck (1976); Murdick, Eckhouse, Moor, and Zimmerer (1976); Paine and Naumes (1974); Rockart (1979); Sproul (1960); and Stevenson (1976).

The evaluation of each key result area in terms of its strategic significance (to effective implementation of grand corporate strategy) is based upon a seven-point rating scale as shown below:

Completely strategically insignificant
Of very little strategic significance

Of somewhat less than average strategic significance
Of average strategic significance
Of somewhat more than average strategic significance
Of very great strategic significance
Of the greatest strategic significance

    The rating scale is a slightly modified version of Steiner's (1969a) measure. Steiner used a six-point scale of values from zero to five for the purpose of evaluating current performance and the future importance of each strategic factor.

    However, the analysis of data on the basis of the strategic significance score of each key result area would be too unwieldy. Besides, the focus of this study is on the strategic significance mix of different organizational functions. Therefore, for each subject firm the strategic significance score is computed for each organizational function by adding up the scores of respective key result areas and dividing the sum by the number of key result areas in that functional category. This approach provides more reliable and logically consistent results than mere rankings of the seven organizational functions in order of importance for each firm.

FIRM SIZE

    Sales volume, total assets, and the number of employees have traditionally been considered as effective size indicators. The authoritative annual Fortune directories rank the top 1,000 U.S. industrial corporations on the basis of their annual sales volume; for this purpose the sales are defined as annual sales revenue inclusive of service and rental revenues but exclusive of dividends, interests, and other nonoperating revenues and excise taxes. Based on this widely accepted definition of sales, the subject firms (the 1,000 largest U.S. industrial incorporations as listed in the 1978 Fortune directory) are classified by the survey respondents into the following three categories as per their sales:

Firm Size	Annual Sales (in millions of dollars)
Small	100–200
Medium	201–599
Large	600 and over

    This classification scheme divides the 1978 Fortune 1,000 firms into three more or less equal groups. The breaking points of

$201 million and $600 million represent the sales of the 688th largest firm (69th percentile) and the 342nd largest firm (34th percentile), respectively.

CATEGORIES OF CORPORATE DIVERSITY

The extent of diversity of a firm's current operations is a function of the success of the degree and type of product-market diversification strategies pursued by the firm in the past. Thus, if a company has pursued the strategy of concentrating on a single business, such a company would be a single business firm. On the other hand, a company with a history of aggressive diversification into new products and markets unrelated to its primary end-product business would be an unrelated busifirm or a conglomerate. Therefore, the concept of corporate diversity is a reflection of a firm's concept of its own strategic posture.

Wrigley (1970) used a random sample of 100 firms from the 1967 Fortune 500 firms and classified these firms into the following four categories of diversity:

1. Single product: no diversification, primary commitment to a single business;

2. Dominant product: primary commitment to a single business and diversification to a small degree;

3. Related product: diversification into new areas concentrically related (by market or technology) to the primary end-product business;

4. Unrelated product: diversification into new areas without regard to such relationships.

Rumelt (1974) modified and expanded Wrigley's classification system and introduced the concept of "specialization ratio" as the primary measure of corporate diversity. He defined specialization ratio

as the proportion of a firm's revenues that is attributable to its largest discrete product-market activity. A "discrete business" (or product-market activity) is one that is strategically independent of the firm's other businesses in that basic changes in its nature and scope can be made without meeting constraints imposed by other of the firm's businesses and without materially affecting the operation and strategic direction of other of the firm's businesses. [P. 29]

The categories of corporate diversity developed for this study are derived from Wrigley (1970) and Rumelt (1974). Figure 3.1 provides a flow diagram that describes the process of categorizing a firm. The survey respondents (senior executives) were therefore asked to indicate the extent of their corporate diversity from a classification of diversity shown in Appendix C (Senior Executive's Questionnaire).

CATEGORIES OF INDUSTRY

The Fortune directories classify the 1,000 largest U.S. industrial corporations into 28 industry groups based on the industry code numbers established by the United States Office of Management and Budget and issued by the Federal Statistical Policy and Standards Office. However, the firms in this study were classified into four broad categories on the basis of their principal industry (representing the largest percentage of company sales) as shown below:

1. Consumer nondurable goods industries
2. Consumer durable goods industries
3. Capital goods industries
4. Produces goods (raw materials, components, and supplies) industries

The above classification scheme is derived from Khandwalla (1977) and Schoeffler, Buzzell, and Heany (1974). The survey respondents were therefore asked to identify their industry from among the above four categories.

CATEGORIES OF PRODUCTION SYSTEM

The following classification system, developed by Woodward (1965), is used in the study:

Unit and small-batch production
Large-batch and mass production
Continuous-process production

As mentioned earlier in Chapter 2 the reason for choosing Woodward's production system classification scheme is that it is the least abstract and can easily be explained. Therefore, it was hoped the practicing executives would be able to identify their predominant production system without the need for a lengthy explanation of terms used.

FIGURE 3.1

The Process of Assigning Corporate Diversity Categories on the
Basis of Specialization Ratio and the Nature of Diversification

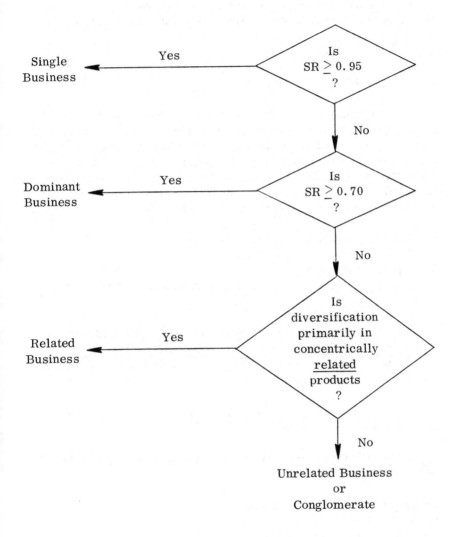

SR = specialization ratio

Source: Derived from Richard P. Rumelt, Strategy, Structure, and Economic Performance (Boston: Harvard Business
School, 1974), p. 30

CATEGORIES OF ORGANIZATIONAL STRUCTURE

In Chapter 2 the relevant literature pertaining to the strategy-structure relationship was reviewed. Some corporate growth and development paradigms developed by the Harvard researchers were also briefly described earlier. Analyses of the history of U.S. and West European industrial enterprises have shown a gradual but unmistakable evolution of organizations from functional to multidivisional forms. With an increase in the volume and diversity of product-market activities, successful firms have tended to make suitable changes in the design of their organizational structure.

A recent effort at building a conceptual model of different types of organization is exemplified by Galbraith and Nathanson (1978). Their model of five organizational types relates the organizational form to strategy and structural characteristics as outlined in Table 3.1. Besides structure and strategy, the model also describes some other characteristics (for example, research and development, interunit and market relations, performance measurement, leader style, and control) of each organizational form. Galbraith and Nathanson (1978) point out the following:

> The firm changes all these characteristics when moving from one form to another. Collectively, the characteristics constitute the way of life of the organization. They form an integrated whole which fit together to permit effective implementation of the respective strategies. When the organization changes strategies, these characteristics must be disengaged, realigned, and reconnected. This change constitutes a metamorphosis. [P. 120]

Rumelt (1974, pp. 33-40) developed the following five categories of organizational structure:

Functional
Functional with one or more product divisions or subsidiaries
Product division
Geographic division
Holding company

Rumelt's classification system was used in this study (see Appendix C) to enable survey respondents to identify their firm's organizational structure.

TABLE 3.1

Strategy and Structural Characteristics of Five Organizational Types

Type of Organization	Strategy	Organization
1. Simple	Single product	Simple functional
2. Functional	Single product and vertical integration	Central functional
3. Holding	Growth by acquisition and unrelated diversity	Decentralized profit centers around divisions; small headquarters
4. Multidivisional	Related diversity of product lines; internal growth; some acquisition	Decentralized product or area division profit centers
5. Global	Multiple products in multiple countries	Decentralized profit centers around worldwide product or area divisions

Source: Derived from Jay R. Galbraith and Daniel A. Nathanson, Strategy Implementation: The Role of Structure and Process (St. Paul, Minn.: West, 1978), p. 118.

PERCEIVED ENVIRONMENTAL UNCERTAINTY

The definition and operational measure of perceived environmental uncertainty is adopted from Miles and Snow (1978). According to Miles and Snow, "perceived environmental uncertainty refers . . . to the predictability of conditions in the organization's environment" (p. 195). It was measured in this study on the basis of the perceived environmental uncertainty questionnaire (see Appendix C), which uses a seven-point rating scale. The questions

corresponded to six major sectors of the industrial organization's environment: (1) relations with raw material suppliers, (2) competitors' product price, quality and design changes, (3) customer demand, (4) relations with financial suppliers, (5) relations with governmental regulatory agencies, and (6) relations with labor unions.

These environmental dimensions were suggested by
previous theory and research by Dill (1958), Katz and
Kahn (1966), Lawrence and Lorsch (1967) and Thompson (1967). [Pp. 195-96]

CONCLUSION

The purpose of this chapter has been to explain the definitions
and measures of eight key concepts underlying this study's conceptual
framework. The schemes for categorizing grand corporate strategy,
firm size, corporate diversity, industry, production system, and
organizational structure; the schemes for measuring the relative
strategic significance of different organizational functions; and perceived environmental uncertainty have all been explained. Chapter
4 describes the study's conceptual framework and poses and discusses
the study's research questions.

4

CONCEPTUAL
FRAMEWORK

INTRODUCTION

The purpose of this chapter is to describe the conceptual
framework utilized in the study. This chapter will include an overview and a separate discussion for each research question investigated
by the study. As part of an explanation of the nature and objectives of
the study in Chapter 1, a summary form of the conceptual framework
was presented in Figure 1.1 to provide an overview of the whole
study. The definitions and measures of concepts used in the study
have already been explained in the previous chapter, and the detailed
conceptual framework showing the interrelationships among variables
involved in the study is outlined in Figure 4.1.

OVERVIEW

The basic assumption of this study is that in an industrial firm
the following seven major organizational functions can have significant influence on the effective implementation of the firm's grand
corporate strategy. The seven major organizational functions are
general administration, production/operations, engineering and research and development (R&D), marketing, finance, personnel, and
public and government relations. However, the relative strategic
significance of different organizational functions or the strategic mix
of organizational functions would be different for firms pursuing different grand corporate strategies. Since no two firms are exactly
alike (even for firms pursuing identical grand corporate strategies),
we would expect that the strategic mixes of organizational functions
would be different for firms of different size, with different degrees

FIGURE 4.1

The Conceptual Framework Showing the Interrelationships between Variables Involved in the Study

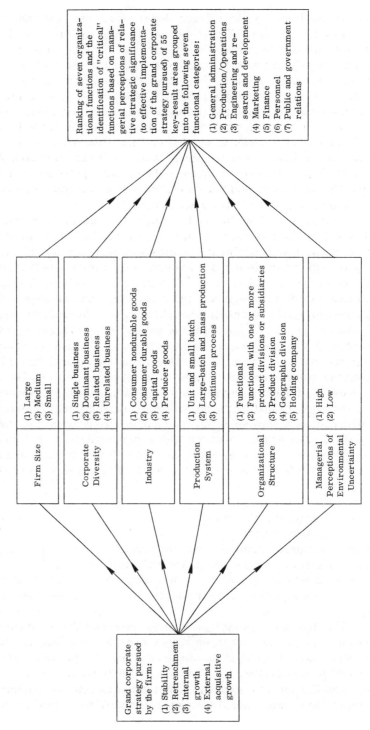

Source: Compiled by the authors.

of corporate diversity, in different industries, with different production systems, with different organizational structures, and with
different managerial perceptions of environmental uncertainty. The
study probes the relative strategic significance of each of the seven
functional tasks for the effective implementation of the grand corporate strategy pursued by the firm. This would help us to understand the nature in which the influence of all seven organizational functions in a firm combine. The particular combination of the influences
of all the seven functions is what we call the strategic mix of organizational functions. The functional tasks' influence-mix approach
to the study of corporate strategy is the central approach of this study.
Godiwalla, Meinhart, and Warde (1979) have developed a similar concept, which they call a "strategicity index."

This book is about theory building rather than theory testing,
and therefore the conceptual frameworks have limited attributes of
explicability, generalizability, replicability, and predictability. This
study is exploratory in that the attempt is to develop a better understanding of the concept of corporate strategy. First, the intent is to
establish the relationships between grand corporate strategies and
the strategic mixes of organizational functions. Second, the study
will attempt to identify the nature of the influence of size, corporate
diversity, industry type, production system, organization structure,
and perceived environmental uncertainty on the interrelationships
among the grand corporate strategies pursued and the relative importance of different functional tasks. Thus, the aim of this study is
to provide understanding rather than to provide generalizations or
predict causality between different variables involved in the study.

In the process of corporate strategy formulation and implementation, there emerges a means-ends chain of relationships and a
hierarchy of different phases, as shown by Paine and Naumes (1974).

Ends: Basic corporate mission
         Corporate objectives
         Corporate goals
Means: Corporate strategies and policies
         Corporate organizational structure
         Functional objectives, goals, strategies, policies, programs,
           roles, tasks, and structures

The first three phases provide the ends that the organization
seeks to achieve; the last three phases provide the means for achieving these ends. Corporate strategies and policies provide a blue-
print, or plan of action, for achieving organizational goals, which are
made specific and time-bound. Corporate strategies and policies
influence the organizational structure that provides a medium within

TABLE 4.1

Four Stages in Long-range Profit Planning

Phase 1: Corporate profit objectives
  Analysis of record of operations
  Establishment of standards for future profits
  Projection of present operations
  Measurement of extent of need for new products
  Preparation of five- and ten-year corporate objectives of sales,
    profits, and capital requirements for present and new products
Phase 2: Proprietary directions for corporate growth
  Audit of corporate skills, resources, and limitations
  Position of company in its total industry structure
  Changing end-use markets, technologies, and competitive integra-
    tion affecting industry structure and company position
  Alternative directions for company evolution and growth
  Selection of most proprietary directions to maintain and optimize
    profits
Phase 3: Planning new products
  Selection of product fields to fulfill corporate objectives of Phase 1
    within selected directions of Phase 2
  Determination of approach to new fields—by acquisition, internal
    research, joint ventures, and so on
  Programming of specific product lines
  Scheduling of realization of new products in relation to financial
    and management feasibility
Phase 4: Programming requirements of business functions
  Marketing—focusing market development plans and programming
    (products, merchandising, pricing, field sales, and so on) on
    consumer requirements
  Organization—scheduling, recruitment, and development of man-
    power requirements (management, other personnel) to staff long-
    range programs
  Research and development—relating research and development to
    divisional and corporate present-product maintenance and new-
    product realization
  Manufacturing—scheduling further development of present and new
    plants and low-cost equipment programs
  Financial—budgeting of capital requirements and development of
    financial resources
  Planning of other requirements

Source: William E. Hill, "Planning for Profits: A Four-Stage Method," California Management Review 1 (Spring 1959): 32.

which the corporate strategies are deployed. The last phase provides for the processes and structures involved in the detailed implementation of corporate strategies pursued by the organization.

Some 20 years ago, Hill (1959) outlined four phases of preparing a long-range profit plan (see Table 4.1) In the last phase, he laid down the planning requirements of each of the five principal business functions, namely, marketing, organization, R&D, manufacturing, and finance.

Murdick (1964) advocated corporate planning based on a planning matrix consisting of three orthogonal vectors (or planning approaches)— product planning, elements-of-cost planning, and functional planning— with the "corporate mold" providing the basic shape or limitations of the planning matrix. Thus, for every product it is expected that planning would be done by functions and cost elements with the corporate-level planning laying down the principles and policies that could provide rational and ethical guidelines for deciding upon taking action to attain company objectives and goals. For functional planning the tasks were identified as marketing, engineering and research, production, employee relations, and finance.

According to Vancil and Lorange (1975) the process of formulation of corporate strategy, business strategy, and functional strategy takes place at three organizational levels—the headquarters, division, and department, respectively.

> The planning processes leading to the formulation of these strategies can be labeled in parallel fashion as corporate planning, business planning, and functional planning. . . . In functional planning, the departments develop a set of feasible action programs to implement division strategy, while the division selects—in the light of its objectives—the subset of programs to be executed and coordinates the action programs of the functional departments. Strategy formulation involves selecting objectives and goals for each functional area (marketing, production, finance, research, and so on) and determining the nature and sequence of actions to be taken by each area to achieve its objectives and goals. Programs are the building blocks of strategic functional plans. [P. 82]

Hofer (1973) also describes the "strategy set" as consisting of a firm's objectives, strategy, and functional policies.

The strategic planning phase does not end with the formulation of strategy. It has been said that to achieve any objective, one has to make a plan and make that plan work. A plan or a strategy, un-

FIGURE 4.2

The Formulation-Implementation Line

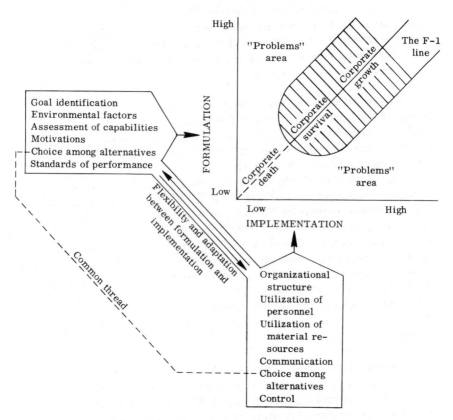

Source: R. Hal Mason, Jerome Harris, and John McLaughlin, "Corporate Strategy: A Point of View." Copyright 1971 by the Regents of the University of California. Reprinted from California Management Review, vol. 13, no. 3, p. 11, by permission of the Regents.

til it is properly implemented, remains nothing but pious intentions, laudable aspirations, or virtuous ends. Therefore, a strategy or a plan of action in and of itself is not capable of self-implementation. Thus, strategy implementation is as important as strategy formulation. In fact, most of the issues pertaining to implementation are interrelated with formulation. Learned, Christensen, Andrews, and Guth (1969) observe,

> In real life the processes of formulation and implementa-
> tion are intertwined. Feedback from operations gives
> notice of changing environmental factors to which strat-
> egy should be adjusted. The formulation of strategy is
> not finished when implementation begins. [P. 571]

Mason, Harris, and McLaughlin (1971) have developed a framework based on the dual aces of strategy formulation and implementation. The conceptual scheme illustrated in Figure 4.2 indicates the
funnel concept and shows the many different elements that enter into
the formulation and implementation of corporate strategy. It also indicates that a firm could be subjectively placed on the Formulation-
Implementation (F-I) line at the point of convergence of the subjec-
tive ratings (high or low) of its strategy-formulation and strategy-
implementation processes. If a firm is positioned farther out on the
line (high ratings for both formulation and implementation), it is more
likely to be a growing and successful firm.

According to Steiner and Miner (1977) "implementation encompasses all functions of management, of both strategic and operational
management" (p. 608). They identified four important characteristics
of policy/strategy implementation.

> First, it is clear that the focus is on design and integra-
> tion of major mechanisms, philosophies, structures and
> personal interrelationships. Second, many different dis-
> ciplines are involved in the design, operation and use of
> integrating systems. Third, conflicts inevitably arise
> and must be solved. . . . Fourth, the discharge of re-
> sponsibilities listed requires the exercise of all func-
> tions of management. [P. 609; emphasis added]

Bobbitt, Randolph, and Ford (1980) observe that past research
studies have provided enough evidence to conclude that variations in
organizational structure can be explained by variations in such contextual factors as size, technology, environment, age, ownership,
and employee characteristics. They further argue that by treating
organizational structure as a direct function of choice of a firm's
management, it is conceivable to view structure as the consequence
of a determinable decision-making process. Structure may be viewed
as one of the consequences of an organizational decision problem.

Thus, the designing of the organization structure merely sets
a stage for organizational implementation of strategy in a very broad
sense. The development of functional goals, strategies, and policies
is necessary to make sure that the corporate strategy is implemented
at all levels in the organization. The extent of formalization of func-

tional policies is bound to vary with the size, diversity, and complexity of the firm. Glueck (1976) points out the following:

> Companies have policies about every major aspect of the firm (operations, finance, marketing, etc.) as well as general management. . . . The minimal policies which must be developed are the key functional decisions necessary in the following areas: (1) operations, (2) finance and accounting, (3) personnel, (4) marketing and logistics, and (5) research and development. [P. 234]

Godiwalla, Meinhart, and Warde (1979) provided an operational conceptual framework for the study of the dynamics of functional management strategies in the firm's corporate strategy. Their study has developed the root concept of the mix of influence of strategies for corporate strategy. Their "functional managements influence-mix" approach underscores the root concept.

According to Hake (1974), the preparation of an overall corporate plan requires that a firm be divided into the separate planning areas of marketing, finance, product development, production, organization, and manpower and that a plan be prepared for each such area.

Functional specialization in business organization dates back to the time when people perceived distinct advantages in operationalizing the concepts of specialization and division of labor in all areas of human activity. It also provides for an effective device to obviate the problems inherent to our "bounded rationality" (March and Simon 1958). Moreover, since every functional task enacts its own relevant subenvironment (Weick 1969, 1977), the problem of effective management of the organization-environment interaction for the organization as a whole is broken down into certain specific manageable components, each of which is dealt with in a more specialized and competent manner.

It is also important to bear in mind that divisionalization (on product or geographic lines) of an organization structure does not do away with the functional management concept. On the contrary, it adds another layer of functional managers to each division. Similarly, the matrix form involving project or product management creates another function (of liaison or coordination) within the general management category. The functional management concept is therefore very much an organizational reality and furnishes a useful approach to the study of many organizational problems and also to the study of grand corporate strategy.

The strategic significance of each of the seven organizational functions in this study is not directly determined through managerial perceptions. It is, on the other hand, derived from the managerial perceptions of the strategic significance of key result areas in each of the functional tasks. These key result areas reflect nothing but the functional goals, strategies, and policies necessary for effective implementation of corporate strategy.

It is a concept of this study that the strategic significance of key result areas in different functional tasks is different for each of the four grand corporate strategies. However, it is recognized that these relationships are influenced by a vast variety of organizational and environmental variables. The "total" theory to explain and predict such relationships in terms of the influence of all possible mediating variables cannot be developed on the basis of our existing knowledge. All mediating variables are not of equal importance, nor are they all relevant to the study's research objectives. Therefore, the influence of only the six mediating variables (size, corporate diversity, industry, production system, organizational structure, and perceived environmental uncertainty) on the interrelationships between the effective implementation of grand corporate strategy and the relative strategic significance of the key result areas in the different functional tasks has been made the subject and scope of this study. Besides, the influence of these mediating or contextual variables has been described by the literature to be highly significant in a study of this nature. The underlying assumptions of the theory of this study have been derived from the conceptual discussion covered earlier in this subsection along with the literature reviewed earlier in Chapter 2.

GRAND CORPORATE STRATEGY AND RELATIVE STRATEGIC SIGNIFICANCE OF DIFFERENT ORGANIZATIONAL FUNCTIONS

Glueck (1976) concludes from Steiner's (1969a) study of the strategic factors for current and future business success that "the crucial aspects of strategy that need to be evaluated are (1) Management quality and development, (2) Environmental appraisal, especially market tidings, and (3) Financial return" (p. 265). Therefore, Steiner found general management, marketing, and finance to be strategically significant organizational functions. Godiwalla, Meinhart, and Warde (1979), on the other hand, identified marketing, finance, and production as the three functional managements that had the greatest influence upon the overall corporate strategy. However, they excluded administration or general management from their definition of functional managements, although they did measure its influence upon corporate strategy.

The firm's grand corporate strategy (both past and current) determines the nature of the firm's relevant environment and the resulting organizational states. It also suggests the range of viable options for the firm's organization and management. Allen (1972) found that the environmental requirements, organizational choices, and the resulting organizational states were significantly different for high performing conglomerates and vertically integrated companies. In his research study of corporate acquisitions, Kitching (1967) found that finance had the highest payoff in all types of mergers except one (horizontal mergers—where marketing had the highest payoff followed very closely by finance). Besides, in the case of finance it was easiest to release synergy in all types of mergers except concentric technology mergers. Heau (1976) identified production and finance to be the critical functions for firms pursuing vertical integration and conglomerate diversification. Respectively, Miles and Snow's (1978) typology of organizations indicated that each organization type has its own strategy for responding to the environment and has a particular combination of technology, structure, and management process, which appears to be consistent with its strategy.

These research studies did not address the basic research question of this study: Is the relative importance of different functional tasks different for firms pursuing different grand corporate strategies? However, the available literature does seem to indicate that the senior executives of industrial firms pursuing different grand corporate strategies would have different perceptions about the relative importance of different functions in their firms. Research Question 1 (outlined in the following) seeks to develop a normative framework of effectively prioritizing the strategic organizational functions for the different grand corporate strategies.

Research Question 1: Is the relative strategic significance of the seven organizational functions different for firms pursuing varying grand corporate strategies?

STRATEGY, SIZE, AND STRATEGIC MIXES OF ORGANIZATIONAL FUNCTIONS

Steiner (1969a) did not analyze the strategic factors for business success differently for firms of varying size. Godiwalla, Meinhart, and Warde (1979) found finance to be the "strategic functional management" for large-size firms (sales exceeding $250 million) and marketing to be the "significantly strategic functional management" for both small and medium-size firms. Again, they excluded general management from the definition of functional managements.

According to the organization theory literature, size of the organization has a significant influence on the various strategic and structural variables. In most cases size may be a function of age, the organization's past strategies and performance, and the stage of the organizational life cycle. Size is also interrelated with the structure of the firm's industry as is also the firm's technology and capital intensity. Size also affects the environmental complexity, the organization's structural design, and the management processes that deal with the complexity and uncertainty. The organization theory literature reviewed in Chapter 2 emphasizes the importance of size as a crucial contextual variable in any corporate strategy research. Research evidence seems to indicate that even for firms pursuing identical grand corporate strategies there would be differences in the managerial perceptions of the strategic mixes of organizational functions in firms of different size. Therefore, Research Question 2 seeks to establish the relationship between the type of grand corporate strategy pursued and the identity of functional areas perceived to be strategically significant for effective strategy-implementation in firms of different size.

Research Question 2: For firms pursuing a particular grand corporate strategy, is the relative strategic significance of the seven organizational functions different for firms of varying size?

STRATEGY, CORPORATE DIVERSITY, AND
STRATEGIC MIXES OF ORGANIZATIONAL
FUNCTIONS

Rumelt (1974) examined the relationship between diversification strategy and organization structure and the association between these two key variables and economic performance in large U.S. industrial corporations. Other researchers who like Rumelt were inspired by Chandler's strategy-structure thesis have also studied the impact of corporate diversity on organizational structure and performance.

A high degree of corporate diversity (itself the result of past strategies and performance) means that the organization is simultaneously operating in many different product-market domains. Khandwalla (1977) points out that "typically but not exclusively, diversified organizations tend to have highly variegated environments" (p. 377). The degree of corporate diversity is also related to the organization's internal structure, decision-making processes, environmental complexity and uncertainty, and the nature of boundary-spanning activities.

Kitching (1967) in his study of firms (45 percent of which were conglomerates—unrelated business firms) following external acquisitive growth strategies found effective management of the finance function to be crucial to the success of mergers.

FIGURE 4.3

Strategy Typology

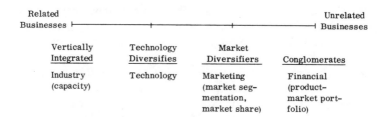

Allen (1972) found that high-performing conglomerates (unrelated business firms) and vertically integrated firms (probably dominant business firms) were faced with different organizational choices and the resulting organizational states.

Fouraker and Stopford (1968) found that organizations pursuing a multinational growth strategy tend to have a highly diversified domestic business with proved R&D leadership.

Heau (1976) observes the following:

> Corporate structure in terms of corporate staff, information flow and corporate culture is presumably related to strategy defined in terms of product relatedness. The more related the businesses (vertical integration being the extreme case) the larger the corporate staff, the more operation-oriented the information flow and the more industry-minded top management. The more unrelated the businesses (conglomerates being here the other extreme), the smaller the corporate staff, the more financially-oriented the information flow and the corporate structure. [P. 10]

For each class of firms, the corporate culture or the orientation of top management was identified as shown in Figure 4.3.

With the increasing trend toward multiplant operations, especially in large multiindustry and multinational firms, the benefits of financial synergy seem to outweigh the economies of scale in production, marketing, and management. According to Pohl (1973), there is a noticeable trend toward an increase in direct involvement of the chief financial officers in the strategic issues handled by the top management.

In Miles and Snow's (1978) typology of organizations, each type has its own strategy. Thus, for example, "defenders" organizations are risk-avert outside their narrow product-market domains, whereas "analyzers" organizations pursue growth strategies in concentrically related areas. One would, therefore, expect to find differences in the structural characteristics, corporate diversity, and management processes in these two types of organizations.

However, no research seems to have focused on identifying the strategic mixes of organizational functions for effective implementation of grand corporate strategies in firms with different degrees of corporate diversity. Therefore, for firms pursuing a particular grand corporate strategy, are the strategic mixes of organizational functions different for firms with the varying degrees of corporate diversity? For instance, if we consider two firms pursuing internal growth strategy, one of which is a "single business" firm while the other is a "related business" firm, can we expect their top managers to prioritize their strategic organizational functions in the same or a different manner?

Research Question 3: For firms pursuing a particular grand corporate strategy, is the relative strategic significance of the seven organizational functions different for firms with varying degrees of corporate diversity?

STRATEGY, INDUSTRY, AND STRATEGIC
MIXES OF ORGANIZATIONAL FUNCTIONS

Several research studies have utilized the concept of strategic mixes of organizational functions as a basis to study the content of grand corporate strategy that firms in different industries pursue. Essentially, they evaluate the nature of blending and the degree of importance to the firm's success of certain organizational functional strategies or factors.

Miles and Snow (1978), in their study of the electronics and the food-processing industries, developed the concept of "strategic function," which they define as the "functional area within the organization considered by members of the dominant coalition to be of strategic importance to successful competition in their industry" (p. 196). The chief executives' ranking of the top three strategic functions (by industry) and their counterparts in this study are shown below:

Food Processing	Electronics
Sales and marketing (marketing)	Sales and marketing (marketing)
Production	Research and development (engineering and R&D)
Long-range planning (general administration)	Product engineering (engineering and R&D)

Lawrence and Lorsch (1967b) found that marketing had more influence than production in both container-manufacturing and food-processing firms. This is due to involvement with customers and impact on innovations.

The influence of industry type as a contextual variable may in fact be a composite influence of interaction between size, technological, environmental, and structural contingencies. But industries differ primarily in their environmental complexity and uncertainty, which appear to be relevant and important to the discussion on hand. Therefore, the works of organization theorists like Thompson, Burns and Stalker, Emery and Trist, Lawrence and Lorsch, and Duncan (cited earlier in Chapter 2) provide a strong albeit indirect support for the inclusion of industry type as a mediating variable in any corporate strategy research.

In the absence of any multiple industry studies, it is not possible to test a specific hypothesis. Therefore, Research Question 4 presents an area of inquiry: Is the functional tasks' strategic significance mix for a particular grand corporate strategy different for different industries? The question aims at analyzing interindustry comparisons and contrasts.

Research Question 4: For firms pursuing a particular grand corporate strategy, is the relative strategic significance of the seven organizational functions different for firms in varying industries?

STRATEGY, PRODUCTION SYSTEM, AND
STRATEGIC MIXES OF ORGANIZATIONAL FUNCTIONS

Technology (or the type of production system employed by a firm) and its relationship to other key organizational and environmental variables have been the subject of numerous empirical studies in organizational theory. In one of the earliest studies of this kind, Woodward (1965) examined the relationship between technology (production system) and organizational structure. The Woodward study also tried to identify the "critical function" for each type of production system. She classified the types of production systems into three broad categories and identified the critical function (or strategically significant functional area) for each type of production system.

Types of Production System	Critical Function
Unit and small batch	Development (engineering and research and development)
Large batch and mass manufacturing	Production
Process	Marketing

According to Woodward (1965), for each type of production system "there seemed to be one function that was central and critical in that it had the greatest effect on success and survival" (p. 128). As far as the applicability of Woodward's findings to this study is concerned, two points need to be made: Woodward included only three functions, and she did not distinguish between the firms pursuing different grand corporate strategies, which although irrelevant to her study, is the main point of this study.

Godiwalla, Meinhart, and Warde (1979) define a functional management strategy group to be strategic if it is most important to the firm's overall corporate strategy. Their results show that in firms employing "unit and small batch" type of production, systems marketing is the significantly strategic functional management. This inference was also the case for firms whose predominant type of production system was large batch and mass manufacturing. But for firms having a process type of production, it was found that marketing was the significantly strategic functional management.

There are other studies regarding technology and how it can be used in the study of an organization's grand corporate strategy. Kitching (1967) found technology to be a function in which it was easiest to generate synergy in concentric technological mergers. Heau (1976) identified engineering and R&D as the critical function for firms pursuing growth strategy of concentric technology diversification. Perrow (1970) classified organizations into four technology types and contended that problems faced by each organization type are different and, therefore, the technological and structural requirements of each are also different.

Thompson (1967) developed a series of propositions about organizations with technology as a major determinant of structure. He classified technology into three types: mediating, intensive, and long-linked. He suggested that efforts that are needed for coordinating and controlling an organization's "technical core" are different for each of the three types of technology and, therefore, technology employed by a firm can significantly impact structural dimensions and processes within an organization.

Khandwalla (1974) established a special form of technology-strategy-structure relationships, where the use of mass output technology leads to the pursuit of vertical integration (a growth strategy), which in turn requires certain changes in the organizational structure and decision making.

The organization's primary production system influences the strategic, structural, and scale aspects of the organization. It also affects the strategic mix of organizational functions through its impact on the degree of labor intensity, capital intensity, knowledge intensity (and therefore R&D), and energy intensity.

The type of predominant production system used in an organization determines the nature of its technological subenvironment as does the pattern of an organization's strategic responses to that subenvironment (Lawrence and Lorsch 1967b).

Organization theory literature has highlighted the importance of the type of production system as a crucial contextual variable in a study of this type. Research evidence seems to indicate that even for firms pursuing identical grand corporate strategies there would be differences in the managerial perceptions of the strategic mixes of organizational functions in firms having different production systems. Research Question 5 attempts to examine the relationship between the type of grand corporate strategy pursued and the identity of functional areas perceived to be strategically significant for effective strategy implementation in firms having different production systems.

Research Question 5: For firms pursuing a particular grand corporate strategy, is the relative strategic significance of the seven organizational functions different for firms with varying production systems?

STRATEGY, ORGANIZATIONAL STRUCTURE, AND STRATEGIC MIXES OF ORGANIZATIONAL FUNCTIONS

The interrelationship between diversification strategy and organizational structure has been a subject of many researchers, notably from Harvard Business School. Chandler (1962) showed how different strategies posed different degrees of administrative complexity and, therefore, tended to require different types of organizational structure. In most cases the organization structure was found to follow the growth strategy pursued by the firm.

Fouraker and Stopford (1968), also of Harvard Business School, found that organizations pursuing a multinational growth strategy tend to have decentralized and divisionalized structure and also displayed the ability to produce international general managers capable of controlling and guiding a highly diversified organization in different global environments.

Heau (1976) grouped the firms into four different types of strategy categories and contended that a comparison along their corporate organizational structure would show differing tendencies; in particular, the functions existing at the top would be different for all four types.

Pitts (1977) found systematic structural differences between internal diversifiers and acquisitive diversifiers.

Khandwalla's (1974) study established a special form of technology-strategy-structure relationships where the adoption of mass-output technology leads to the pursuit of vertical integration, which in turn requires certain changes in the organizational structure and decision making.

Miller and Springate (1978) found that in product-divisional organization structures comparable decisions tend to be made at lower levels of the organization than in the functional organizational structures.

Litschert and Bonham (1978) considered the level of organizational slack as a major determinant of the contingent nature of strategy. In their conceptual model of strategy formation, organizational slack as a crucial moderator variable influences the necessary fit between structure and contextual variables and ultimately the causal direction of the strategy-structure relationship.

The "stages of growth and development" theorists (Cannon, Thain, Tuason, Galbraith and Nathanson, and others) have developed conceptual models of the corporate life cycle with distinct stages of corporate development. The strategy and structural characteristics of firms in different stages of growth are different.

The crucial significance of organizational structure in corporate planning emanates primarily from the fact that corporate planning, as the name suggests, is essentially an organizationwide activity rather than something to be done only by the corporate planning staff. The effective implementation of corporate strategies, therefore, requires that the organization structure must fit the firm's planning needs, and also that any planning to be done must recognize the nature of organizational structure. As Koontz (1976) points out, "The organizational structure should be designed to support the accomplishment of goals and the making of decisions to implement strategies" (p. 47). According to Richards (1978), organizational structure is important in the formulation and implementation of strategy

> because the locus of planning, goal setting and decision-
> making is dependent upon the type of structure in which

the planning is done. . . . Additionally, there is a correspondence between the hierarchy of organizational
structure and the hierarchy of strategies. [P. 25]

The relationships between corporate strategy and structural and
administrative decisions (advocated by Chandler, Rumelt, and others)
and the relationships between a firm's structural and administrative
decisions and its environmental complexity and uncertainty (advocated by organization theorists like Burns and Stalker, Woodward,
Lawrence and Lorsch, and others) are gradually emerging into a contingency theory of the firm (Ward 1976) in which the organizational
administration (structure, decision-making process, and so on) is a
function of the firm's strategic choice, which in turn is a function of
the environment and corporate resources.

Literature from both business policy and organization theory,
therefore, seems to indicate that the influence of organizational structure as a mediating or contextual variable would be highly significant
in a study of this nature. Thus, we could expect differences in the
strategic mixes of organizational functions in firms pursuing identical
grand corporate strategies but having different types of organizational
structures. Hence, for Research Question 6 our area of inquiry would
be: For the firms pursuing a particular grand corporate strategy, is
the strategic significance of different organizational functions different for firms with different types of organizational structure? In
other words, if we consider two firms pursuing, say, internal growth
strategy, one of which is organized on functional lines and the other
a product-divisional organization structure, can we expect their top
managers to prioritize their strategic organizational functions in the
same or different manner?

Research Question 6: For firms pursuing a particular grand
corporate strategy, is the relative strategic significance of the seven
organizational functions different for firms with varying types of organizational structures?

STRATEGY, PERCEIVED ENVIRONMENTAL
UNCERTAINTY, AND STRATEGIC MIXES OF
ORGANIZATIONAL FUNCTIONS

Organization-environment interaction has been a favorite theme
of organization theorists for some time. However, only recently have
researchers come to the conclusion that organizations do not respond
in a predictable manner to their given external environments. In
fact, organizations "enact" (Weick 1969, 1977) or shape their own

environments through a series of strategic decisions culminating in an identifiable pattern or configuration. Thus, if we study two corporations over a period of time and identify the strategy set of each corporation, we can determine the nature of their external environments and also ascertain the ways in which the top managers relate their firms to each firm's relevant environments. A firm's product-market domain primarily determines the linkage between the firm and its external environment. The determination of the product-market domain is itself a matter of a series of conscious strategic choices or decisions.

Organization-environment interaction is perhaps one area where the fields of organization theory and strategy-policy show a great deal of similarity. After defining corporate strategy, Aguilar (1967) goes on to add that

> strategy should be responsive to both the risks and opportunities confronting the company in its external environment and the strengths and weaknesses—present and potential—within the firm itself. [P. 4]

According to Taylor (1973), strategic decisions are "concerned with effecting major changes in the 'linkages' between the enterprise and its environment" (p. 37). A firm's grand corporate strategy, therefore, sets the stage for organizational adaptation to its environment.

Lorsch (1973), commenting on the Lawrence and Lorsch (1967) study, states that

> each functional unit (e.g. sales, production, and research) must have internal characteristics consistent with the demands of its particular sector of the total environment [and] the total organization must achieve, in spite of the differentiation among its units the pattern of integration required by the total environment. [P. 132]

According to Hickson, Hinings, Lee, Schneck, and Pennings (1971), "The more a subunit copes with uncertainty, the greater its power within the organization" (p. 220). The source of power, therefore, lies in the subunit's ability to cope effectively with high uncertainty and in its role as a "shock absorber" for the whole organization, assuming that the rest of the organization acknowledges the importance of such a shock-absorbing process.

Salancik, Pfeffer, and Kelly (1974) contend that the source of influence in organizational decision making is determined "through a communication process which serves to define the source of uncertainty and to locate individuals capable of coping with the uncertainty" (p. 55).

Godiwalla, Meinhart, and Warde (1979) utilized Duncan's (1972) framework for studying how chief executives blend their functional management strategies in the context of total organizational environments. They found that firms operating in Duncan's simple-static environment tend to emphasize the internally oriented, functional management strategies like production. However, for other firms operating in Duncan's dynamic-complex environments the externally oriented, functional management strategies, like marketing, were emphasized, while the internally oriented, functional managements were not emphasized.

One might well ask, Is the functional areas' influence-mix approach relevant to the study of organization-environment interaction? The relevance of this approach becomes obvious when one considers each functional area as a specialized internal subsystem organized to interact effectively with its relevant (external) subenvironment. Therefore, the nature of a firm's relevant (or enacted) subenvironments determines the relative strategic importance of different functional tasks. The recognizable pattern of an organization's responses to environmental issues (according to Miles, Snow, and Pfeffer 1974; Child 1972a; and Richards 1973) is determined not so much by the objective characteristics of organization-environment interactions as by the managerial perceptions of the strategic significance of key result areas in different organizational functions.

Miles and Snow (1978) examined the relationship between the managerial perceptions of environmental uncertainty and the relative strategic importance of different organizational functions. They found some support for the contention

> that when the organization faces high environmental uncertainty, it places greater emphasis on externally oriented functions such as market research and product development. . . . Conversely when an organization faces low uncertainty, internally oriented function (such as production) assumes strategic importance. [P. 213]

Therefore, both high- and low-perceived environmental uncertainty tend to produce identifiable but different strategic mixes of organizational functions. When the perceived uncertainty in a subenvironment is high, the functional area responsible for managing the interface with that subenvironment must concentrate on effective avoidance/reduction of critical uncertainties to ensure the firm's survival and growth. Therefore, in the firm's internal power structure and the resource-allocation process that functional area is likely to acquire a commanding position.

However, in this study, perceived environmental uncertainty is not the independent variable. The research evidence cited earlier does not tell us whether for firms pursuing a particular grand corporate strategy, the ranking of organizational functions in terms of their strategic significance would vary by amounts of perceived environmental uncertainty.

Research Question 7: For firms pursuing a particular grand corporate strategy, is the relative strategic significance of the seven organizational functions different for firms with varying perceived environmental uncertainty?

CONCLUSION

The state of our existing knowledge in the field of business policy and corporate strategy precludes us from setting forth with any reasonable degree of certainty "a contingency theory or even a set of limited domain theories" (Steiner and Miner 1977, p. 781; emphasis added). Conceptually and theoretically, as well as empirically, business policy is a newly emerging discipline that highlights the need for more exploratory research in the early stages of its development as the field gradually moves toward conceptual and theoretical maturity. Galbraith (1967), in his controversial book The New Industrial State, points out the following:

> Few subjects of earnest inquiry have been more unproductive than a study of the modern large corporation. The reasons are clear. A vivid image of what should exist acts as a surrogate for reality. Pursuit of the image then prevents pursuit of the reality. [P. 72; emphasis added]

Steiner and Miner (1977) point out that the research in any field generally goes through three distinct phases.

> As research in a field develops it tends to appear first in the form of surveys dealing with practice, attitudes, and intentions; then in the form of correlational or correlational-type analyses relating key variables to each other; and finally in the form of experimental studies that establish causal relationships. The field of policy-strategy is now moving into the second of these phases, although certain of its subareas are still in the initial survey phase. [P. 781; emphasis added]

Therefore, we have a long way to go before we can say with confidence to a top manager, "If your firm has adopted grand corporate

strategy X, is large, is a dominant business undertaking, is a consumer nondurable goods industry, has a continuous process production
system, is organized on product division lines, and if the top management's perception of environmental uncertainty is high, then implementation of your grand corporate strategy X will be more effective
and successful if you closely monitor and evaluate performance in the
key result areas in strategically significant or critical functions Y_1
and Y_2." For we have yet to develop a theory embodying an empirically tested set of normative contingency hypotheses in the area
of effective implementation of different grand corporate strategies.

This study, which is a logical extension, amplification, and re-
finement of similar studies by Steiner (1969a); Godiwalla, Meinhart,
and Warde (1979); and Miles and Snow (1978), raises a set of seven
specific research questions and seeks answers through empirical
analysis. This exploratory study attempts to develop a better understanding of strategic mixes of organizational functions for different
grand corporate strategies and thereby hopes to contribute to the development of the substantive area of policy-strategy.

To conclude, the theoretical background of this study's conceptual framework, derived from the relevant parts of Chapter 2 on
literature review, has been discussed in this chapter, and research
questions in the seven specific areas of study have been presented.
The research methodology, related to the data collection and the data
analyses for investigating the research questions, is presented in the
next chapter.

5

RESEARCH
METHODOLOGY

RESEARCH DESIGN

Research in the field of corporate strategy is conceptually and methodologically more difficult than in other more developed fields. The knowledge about corporate strategy is available in many different forms and styles. Bowman (1974) observes the following:

> Synthesis or design, especially in the policy of an organization, however, requires the consideration of most/many of the aspects of the situation. . . . Many facts about the world and about a firm are important for making decisions about corporate strategy. It is rather difficult to attempt many generalizations . . . in a field as imperfect as corporate strategy. Much of what now exists as an academic field of corporate strategy (and business policy) should probably be thought of as "contingency theory." The ideas, recommendations, or generalizations are rather dependent (contingent) for their truth and their relevance on the specific situational factors. [P. 36; emphasis added]

According to Bowman, there are many different approaches to the understanding and knowledge of corporate strategy (see Figure 5.1). In view of the embryonic nature of the field, his recommendation is to adopt them all.

For this business-policy study, the nature of the policy-strategy area and the current state of its development imposes certain inherent limitations on the choice of appropriate research design. The theory building in this area favors inductive, creative, intensive field research.

FIGURE 5.1

Organized Taxonomy of Approaches to the Understanding and Knowledge of Corporate Strategy

	Less Formal	More Formal
Practice	Cases	History
Methodology	Analytical Approach	Management Science
Theory	Behavioral	Economics

Source: Edward H. Bowman, "Epistemology, Corporate Strategy, and Academe," Sloan Management Review 15 (Winter 1974): 36.

Kerlinger (1973) defines field studies as "ex post facto scientific inquiries aimed at discovering the relationships and interactions among sociological, psychological, and educational variables in real social structures" (p. 405). Since this research study does not involve the manipulation of independent variables, the experimental research (involving laboratory or field experiments) would not be appropriate. Ex post facto research by definition is "systematic empirical inquiry in which the scientist does not have direct control of independent variables because their manifestations have already occurred or because they are inherently not manipulable" (Kerlinger 1973, p. 379). The data for this field study were obtained through the use of survey-type instruments (mail questionnaires).

This study is exploratory in nature and is intended to reveal more fully the relationships among the variables involved. The exploratory type of study "seeks what is rather than predicts relations to be found." Such a study has "three purposes: to discover significant variables in the field situation, to discover relations among variables and to lay the groundwork for later, more systematic and rigorous testing of hypotheses" (Kerlinger 1973, p. 406).

SAMPLE ORGANIZATIONS

The sample organizations for this study consisted of the 1,000 largest U.S. industrial corporations as listed in the 1978 <u>Fortune</u> directory. The list therefore included only manufacturing industries and did not include banking, financial, utilities, transportation, wholesale and retail trade, and other service industries.

DATA COLLECTION PROCEDURES

Many business-policy research studies rely on field surveys for collection of relevant data. Field surveys are normally classified on the basis of the following methods used for obtaining information:

Personal interview
Telephone interview
Mail questionnaire
Controlled observations

The information obtained may or may not be supplemented by the examination and collection of available (secondary) data germane to the study.

A field survey utilizing personal interview was ruled out because of inordinately high costs and the length of time required. Also, the inaccessibility of data sources because of the reluctance on the part of senior executives to grant interviews was an important consideration. A telephone survey was also not practical, since the nature of the study calls for data that cannot be collected by telephone. The wide geographic dispersion of respondents (the top 1,000 U.S. industrial corporations), the nature of the data, and budget and time limitations all dictated a mail survey, which has the additional advantage of providing respondents a guarantee of anonymity and security to respond to questions of a highly confidential nature.

The data for the study were collected through mail questionnaires designed to be filled out by senior executives having adequate familiarity with the firm's overall operations and its business environment. The first draft of the questionnaire was tested for question content, question wording, and response structure among a group of researchers familiar with the problems of field surveys in the area of business policy. After this in-house testing, the questionnaire was revised. This revised questionnaire was retested by administering it to a small pilot sample to ascertain the rate and the quality of response.

In the pilot study (also by mail questionnaire), an attempt was made to determine the respondents' feelings and reactions to the

TABLE 5.1

Things Liked Most and Least about Academic Mail Surveys

	Number of Responses	Percent[c]
Things liked most[a]		
Provides valuable information	21	45.8
Opportunity to help academic community	8	17.2
Displays interest in business/company	7	15.0
Chance to tell company's story	4	9.0
"Feel" for academic thinking	3	6.5
Thought provoking for own company	3	6.5
Total	46	100.0
Things liked least[b]		
Inordinate amount of time to complete/ questionnaire too long	47	46.1
Subject matter not relevant to company	25	24.5
Poor questionnaire	22	21.6
Questions too general	11	10.8
Attitude of researcher	11	10.8
Subject or questionnaire too complex	5	4.9
Total	121	118.7

[a]Respondents were asked, "What two things do you like MOST about academic mail surveys?"

[b]Respondents were asked, "What two things do you like LEAST about academic mail surveys?"

[c]Indicates percent of times mentioned by the 102 respondents.

Source: Ralph M. Gaedeke and Dennis H. Tootelian, "The Fortune '500' List—An Endangered Species for Academic Research," Journal of Business Research 4 (1976): 286.

questioning process and the specific questions in the instrument so that the instrument could then be revised. The intent was to ensure that the respondents understood the meaning and intent of the questions and that the questions themselves were capable of obtaining the information and perceptions sought by the researcher.

The pilot study was necessary to determine the potential for an adequate response rate and to determine the reliability and validity

TABLE 5.2

Importance of Factors Influencing the Response Rate

Factors	Weighted Average[a]	Number of Responses			Total Responses[b]
		Very Important	Somewhat Important	Not Important	
Amount and type of statistical data called for	1.79	80	19	3	102
Stated purpose of survey	1.65	72	21	2	95
Subject matter of survey	1.63	70	23	3	96
Length of questionnaire	1.57	68	21	7	96
Number of open-ended questions	1.29	48	33	13	94
Assurance of confidentiality	1.12	41	30	20	91
Accompanying letter	1.10	32	36	23	91
Sender's reputation or position	1.05	30	45	19	94
Promise to receive survey results	0.78	20	38	36	94

[a]Weighted averages are 2 for very important, 1 for somewhat important, 0 for not important.
[b]Some factors were not marked by the respondents.

Source: Ralph M. Gaedeke and Dennis H. Tootelian, "The Fortune '500' List—An Endangered Species for Academic Research," Journal of Business Research 4 (1976): 287.

of the survey instrument. As Nachmias and Nachmias (1976) point out, "The main problem with mail questionnaires is that of obtaining an adequate response rate. . . . The typical response rate . . . for a mail survey is between 20 and 40 percent" (pp. 107-8). A corporate mail survey of the Fortune 500 companies by Gaedeke and Tootelian (1976) resulted in a response rate of 22 percent of which 20.47 percent accounted for completed questionnaires. In most mail questionnaire surveys in corporate strategy research, the respondents are usually extremely busy and highly paid corporate executives, and the information sought is highly confidential in nature. The response rate in such surveys varies from 20 to 30 percent. In view of these constraints, a response rate of about 25 percent is expected in a study of this nature.

While designing the mail survey, the findings of the research by Gaedeke and Tootelian (1976) were carefully considered. They found that "negative responses toward mail questionnaire surveys were indicated almost three times as frequently as positive ones" (p. 285). Table 5.1 reveals what corporate executives like most and least about academic mail surveys. Their findings also indicate the importance of different factors in influencing the response rate (see Table 5.2); the first four factors listed in the table were found to be especially important. Gaedeke and Tootelian conclude that the findings of their study

> indicate that the Fortune "500" List may be an "endangered species" for academicians. The tendency of academicians has been to exploit this rich base of primary data to the point where few if any, benefits are accruing to the recipients of mail questionnaires. If value is to be derived by the recipient, researchers should drastically reduce the frequency of using the "500" List except for highly pertinent survey research that is clearly of benefit to corporate management. [Pp. 286-87]

The Pilot Study

As stated earlier, various research methodology considerations highlighted the need for a pilot study. The two important objectives of the pilot study were to determine whether the study would generate enough interest among the senior executives to motivate their participation in the survey and to determine the reliability and validity of the survey instrument. In their research on academic mail surveys of Fortune 500 companies, Gaedeke and Tootelian (1976) found that 75 out of 94 (or roughly 80 percent) executive officers considered the sender's reputation or position an important factor in influencing the response rate; and "when the respondents were asked for suggestions for improving academic mail surveys, approximately half of the executive officers favored their screening and approval by colleges, universities, or professional associations" (p. 286). Consequently, institutional sponsorship for this study was obtained from an academic institution.

For the pilot study, 60 industrial firms in the southwest region were picked randomly from the Moody's Industrial and OTC Industrial Manuals. As the pilot study envisaged completion of two long questionnaires from each company, and all participating companies were asked to reveal their identities (participants were not provided with a choice to respond anonymously), the respondents' familiarity with the university was an obviously crucial consideration.

A Xeroxed form letter on official stationery was sent to the chief executive officers (CEOs) of 60 industrial firms individually typed with the CEO's address, individualized salutation, and handwritten signatures of the researchers. Two copies of a six-page questionnaire called the "Corporate Strategy Questionnaire for Senior Executives" accompanied by Xeroxed form cover letters with handwritten signatures of the researchers were also enclosed. The names of the chief executive officers were obtained from the Moody's Industrial and OTC Industrial Manuals. In the cover letter the CEO was asked to have two senior executives of his company familiar with its overall operations and its overall business environment complete the enclosed two copies of the questionnaire independently of each other and return the questionnaires in the enclosed, self-addressed, stamped envelopes. The first mailing yielded only nine returns (15 percent). After a period of seven weeks, a follow-up letter and questionnaires were sent to the CEOs of those companies that had not yet responded. (The cover letters and the questionnaire used in the pilot study are presented in Appendix B.)

The pilot survey resulted in 27 returns (45 percent); four companies declined to participate for various reasons, and in the case of two firms only one completed questionnaire was received. Thus, in the case of 21 companies (35 percent), separate questionnaires were filled out independently by two senior executives. This response rate and the reliability and validity of variables computed from the pilot study data (to be discussed later in this chapter) were thought to be encouraging enough to pursue with the mail questionnaire survey method for the main, nationwide field study.

The purpose was to evaluate the interjudge reliability on the instruments that could be assessed by the degree of agreement between the two executives. Data on the nominally scaled variables were first ordered according to a procedure described by Claypool

TABLE 5.3

Instruments Reliability Scores—Pilot Study
(N = 21 firms and 42 judges)

Variable	Coefficient Alpha	$\mathcal{L}^*$	Product-Moment Correlations	Revised Correlations
Grand strategy	n.a.	17.35[a]	n.a.	n.a.
Size	n.a.	14.17[a]	n.a.	n.a.
Industry	n.a.	5.58[a]	n.a.	n.a.
Production system	n.a.	7.23[a]	n.a.	n.a.
Corporate diversity	n.a.	2.172[c]	n.a.	n.a.
Organizational structure	n.a.	3.905[a]	n.a.	n.a.
PEU	.80	n.a.	.69	n.a.
GADM	.86	n.a.	.63	n.a.
PROD	.94	n.a.	.70	n.a.
ERD	.83	n.a.	.52	n.a.
MKTG	.92	n.a.	.60	n.a.
FIN	.92	n.a.	.44	.80
PERS	.88	n.a.	.36	.70
PGR	.85	n.a.	.48	.73

n.a. = not applicable

[a] $p < .01$.
[b] $p < .05$.
[c] $p < .10$.

Source: Compiled by the authors.

(1975) and then a $\mathcal{L}^*$ (Li and Schucany 1975; Schucany and Frawley 1973) was calculated. (A $\mathcal{L}^*$ shows the amount of agreement within and between groups.) Its distribution can be approximated by the standard normal. Data on intervally scaled variables were analyzed using the Pearson product moment correlation. Coefficient alphas were calculated to assess multiitem scales' internal consistency. The results of these analyses are shown in Table 5.3.

The $\mathcal{L}^*$s for all nominally scaled variables were statistically significant, showing good interjudge agreement. The coefficient

TABLE 5.4

Internal Reliabilities—Main Study
(N = 249)

Variable	Coefficient Alpha
PEU	.80
GADM	.81
PROD	.85
ERD	.81
MKTG	.79
FIN	.73
PERS	.66
PGR	.72

Source: Compiled by the authors.

alphas for all multiitem scales were high for both the pilot and main
studies (see Tables 5.3 and 5.4). Thus, they demonstrate good internal consistency. Most of the intervally scaled variables had acceptable interjudge reliability scores with r's > 0.5 (Cronback 1970).
But three of the functional scores had interjudge correlations of less
than 0.5. Because of this, interjudge correlations on each item were
examined. Items were deleted on which interjudge correlations were
low and new reliability scores were calculated. The new interjudge
correlations were within the acceptable range as shown in Table 5.3.
Based on these results, the revised instruments were concluded to
have good reliability.

Khandwalla (1977) noted that if senior executives (as experts on
their firms) agree, it provides not only a measure of interjudge reliability but also a measure of validity. Additionally, Campbell and
Fiske (1959) and Stone (1978) state that correlation between independent variable measures provides evidence of convergent validity. The
pilot study data, then, provide some evidence that the instruments
are valid.

Snow and Hambrick (1980) argue that it is preferable to measure
an organization's strategy in several ways and not rely on a single
measurement method. Therefore, as an additional validity check on
the grand strategy measure, the latest available annual reports of
40 randomly chosen firms were examined for evidence of strategic

actions. The intent was to examine the congruence between CEO questionnaire responses of a grand strategy type and actual corporate actions. Two judges reviewed the annual reports and attempted to select the grand strategy category reflective of the actions described in the annual report. Of the grand strategies depicted by actions described in the annual reports, 33 matched CEO questionnaire responses. Five failed to match, one could not be categorized, and one firm was deleted because of a recent merger. Agreement was obtained, then, in 83 percent of the cases. These results provide further support for the validity of the grand strategy measure.

The Main Study

The pilot study's outcome necessitated the making of certain changes. The senior executive's identification of his firm's grand corporate strategy was considered very crucial to this study. However, some doubts were raised as to whether the executives would identify their grand strategies in a disinterested manner with complete objectivity, since the terms used to label the grand corporate strategies were essentially value laden. It was, therefore, argued that very likely most executives would identify growth strategies as their grand corporate strategies, and almost no executive would admit that his firm pursues a retrenchment strategy. Accordingly, most executives would identify grand corporate strategies that they perceive as desirable or respectable rather than grand corporate strategies actually being pursued by their firms. This might give rise to an incongruity between their identification of grand corporate strategies and their stated perceptions of relative strategic significance of different functional tasks. Also, this possible incongruity arising from a response bias could raise serious doubts about the validity of the research findings. To avoid a potential response bias, the survey instrument used in the pilot study was divided into two separate questionnaires.

The first questionnaire, called the Chief Executive Officer's Questionnaire, consisted of a one-page question about the grand corporate strategy pursued by the firm that was to be answered by the CEO himself. The second questionnaire, called the Senior Executive's Questionnaire, was to be filled out by a senior executive familiar with the firm's overall operations and its overall business environment. It was thought this would greatly reduce the risk of incongruity between the respondents' assertions (about their grand corporate strategies) and perceptions (of various aspects of their organizations and environments).

Another minor change was made in the question dealing with industry classification. One of the respondents had made a telephone

TABLE 5.5

Analysis of Return Rates

	Percent Returned
Two completed questionnaires received (usable)	249/1,000 = 24.9
Two completed questionnaires received (unusable)	8/1,000 = 0.8
Only one (either the Chief Executive Officer's Questionnaire or the Senior Executive's Questionnaire) completed questionnaire received (unusable)[a]	4/1,000 = 0.4
Unwilling to participate in the survey (nonreturned questionnaires):	
Because of corporate policy of not participating in academic mail surveys	19/1,000 = 1.9
For other reasons	10/1,000 = 1.0
Overall return rate[b]	290/1,000 = 29.0

[a]In case of anonymously completed questionnaires, each of these two questionnaires might possibly be from the same company.

[b]It is important to recognize the possibility that some of the firms that did not respond may, in fact, have been following their company policies of not responding to any questionnaires.

Source: Compiled by the authors.

call to determine what exactly was meant by the term capital goods industry. Therefore, the question was modified to include two examples of products from a capital goods industry.

The next step in this process was the Xeroxing and mailing of a form letter on official stationery individually typed with the CEO's address, individualized salutation, and handwritten signatures of the researchers. This letter was sent to the chief executive officers of the 1,000 largest U.S. industrial corporations listed in the 1978 Fortune Directory. Included were a copy each of the Chief Executive Officer's Questionnaire and the Senior Executive's Questionnaire and a self-addressed, stamped envelope. (The cover letter and the two survey instruments are presented in Appendix C.) The names and company addresses of the CEOs were obtained from the Standard & Poor's Register of Corporations, Directors and Executives (1978) and the Dun & Bradstreet Million Dollar Directory, 1978 (1978).

TABLE 5.6

Characteristics of the Sample
(N = 249)

	Percent
Grand corporate strategy pursued	
Stability	11.65
Internal growth	41.77
External acquisitive growth	38.55
Retrenchment	8.03
Firm size (annual sales revenue)	
$200 million and less	24.10
$201 million to $599 million	33.73
$600 million and over	42.17
Corporate diversity	
Single-business firms	11.24
Dominant-business firms	22.09
Related-business firms	46.59
Unrelated-business firms	20.08
Predominant production system	
Unit and small batch production	16.47
Large batch and mass production	55.42
Continuous process production	28.11
Principal industry	
Consumer nondurable goods industries	29.32
Consumer durable goods industries	13.65
Capital goods industries	24.50
Producer goods industries	32.53
Firm organizational structure	
Functional	11.24
Functional with one or more product divisions or subsidiaries	22.89
Product division	44.58
Geographic division	12.85
Holding company	8.44

Source: Compiled by the authors.

Of the 1,000 companies asked to participate in the study, the response indicated an overall return rate of 29 percent (see Table 5.5). The survey resulted in a sample of 249 usable questionnaires (25 percent). The sample characteristics (profile of the companies responding) are presented in Table 5.6. There were no follow-ups on the main study, because it was thought that a response rate of 25 percent yielding 249 usable questionnaires was sufficient for data analysis purposes.

A total of 29 senior executives declined to participate because of corporate policy or for other reasons; the relevant excerpts from some of their letters are reproduced in Appendix D. Many responding firms enclosed a copy of their annual report; some even sent a copy of their Form 10-K Report to the Securities and Exchange Commission.

RESEARCH QUESTIONS

The research questions developed from the conceptual framework discussed earlier in Chapter 4 are presented below:

Research Question 1: Is the relative strategic significance of the seven organizational functions different for firms pursuing varying grand corporate strategies?

Research Question 2: For firms pursuing a particular grand corporate strategy, is the relative strategic significance of the seven organizational functions different for firms of varying size?

Research Question 3: For firms pursuing a particular grand corporate strategy, is the relative strategic significance of the seven organizational functions different for firms with varying degrees of corporate diversity?

Research Question 4: For firms pursuing a particular grand corporate strategy, is the relative strategic significance of the seven organizational functions different for firms in varying industries?

Research Question 5: For firms pursuing a particular grand corporate strategy, is the relative strategic significance of the seven organizational functions different for firms with varying production systems?

Research Question 6: For firms pursuing a particular grand corporate strategy, is the relative strategic significance of the seven organizational functions different for firms with varying types of organizational structures?

Research Question 7: For firms pursuing a particular grand corporate strategy, is the relative strategic significance of the seven organizational functions different for firms with varying perceived environmental uncertainty?

DATA ANALYSIS PROCEDURES

After the strategic significance scores for each of the seven organizational functions (computed by adding up the scores of key result areas in a particular function and dividing the sum by the number of key result areas in that particular functional category) were obtained, the firms were grouped on the basis of their grand corporate strategy. Within each group, mean strategic significance scores were computed for each of the seven organizational functions. Similar mean scores (grand means) were also computed for the entire sample of 249 firms. In each strategy group, as also for the overall sample, the seven organizational functions were ranked by their mean strategic significance scores. The slippage test recommended by Conover (1971) was used to determine if the functional scores were distributed similarly in each grand corporate strategy grouping. The differences in mean values within each group were ascertained by paired t-tests in the form of approximate least significant difference (LSD) tests. Additionally, for each group an F-ratio was calculated, using the repeated measures design, from an analysis of variance (one-way classification by organizational function) for the strategic significance score (grand mean). This F-ratio indicates the magnitude of differences between mean scores of different functions in each strategy group.

The approximate LSD tests and the one-way analysis of variance (AOV) as a repeated measures design were used separately for each of the four strategy types as also for the overall sample. Additionally, F-ratios were also calculated from an AOV (one-way classification of 249 firms by grand corporate strategy) for the mean strategic significance scores of each of the seven different organizational functions. These F-ratios would indicate whether there do exist significant differences among the mean strategic significance scores of each function attributable to the grand corporate strategies. These analyses provided pertinent data for testing Research Question 1.

Data aggregated by each of the four strategy types were further analyzed by size, corporate diversity, industry, production system, organizational structure, and perceived environmental uncertainty and were subjected to the same analysis described earlier. Thus, analysis of subject firms (for the purpose of testing Research Question 2) by firm size yielded a 3 × 4 factorial design of firm size × grand corporate strategy. Within each of the 12 cells of that factorial design, the seven organizational functions were ranked by their mean strategic significance scores. Within each cell, the differences in mean values were ascertained by paired t-tests in the form of approximate LSD tests. For row mean scores in each size group, an F-ratio was calculated from an AOV (one-way classification by organizational function) in the nature of a repeated measures design. F-ratios were also computed from an AOV (one-way classification of 249 firms by size) for the mean strategic significance scores of each of the seven functions. And finally, F-ratios were computed from an unweighted AOV (two-way classification of 249 firms by size and grand corporate strategy) for the mean strategic significance scores of each of the seven functions. These analyses provided pertinent data for testing Research Question 2.

Similarly, Research Question 3 was tested by analyzing a 4×4 factorial design of Strategy $\times$ Corporate Diversity; Research Question 4 by a 4×4 factorial design of Strategy $\times$ Industry; Research Question 5 by a 4×3 factorial design of Strategy $\times$ Production System; and Research Question 6 by a 4×5 factorial design of Strategy $\times$ Organizational Structure. However, for the purpose of testing Research Question 7, the subject firms were divided into three classes: (1) firms with high perceived environmental uncertainty, (2) firms with medium perceived environmental uncertainty, and (3) firms with low perceived environmental uncertainty. These three groupings of perceived environmental uncertainty (PEU) scores were obtained using hierarchical cluster analysis. Research Question 7 was tested by using a 4×3 factorial design of Strategy $\times$ PEU.

The analysis of data on the lines indicated above has provided an effective way for seeking answers to the seven research questions raised in this study. The strategic significance mixes of organizational functions were thus determined by using observational ranking and approximate least significant difference tests along with the analysis of variance. Kendall and Buckland (1971) define a least significant difference test as

> a test for comparing mean values arising in analysis of variance. It is an extension of the standard t-test for the difference between two specified mean values. Because the tests between pairs are not independent the error rate is difficult to assess exactly. [P. 83]

The theoretical limits and the critical values of the LSD test[1] are the same as those of a t-test.

In view of the objectives of this study and the nature of the data involved, the LSD test seems best suited for data analysis. A valid LSD test can be constructed notwithstanding unequal sample size in different cells of a factorial design. Other alternative tests (namely, Duncan's new multiple-range tests, Tukey's W-procedure or honestly significant difference (HSD) procedure, and Student-Newman-Keuls' test) only provide an approximate test statistic for unequal sample size. The LSD test, on the other hand, provides an exact statistic for unequal sample size. A question might arise as to the appropriateness of this parametric test, since most of the data for this study would be collected using the Likert scale involving nonnormal distributions. However, the LSD test is still valid, as per the Central Limit Theorem; as long as the distribution of observations satisfies certain assumptions (like σ is finite), then the distribution of $\overline{X}$ would be approximately normal for large sample sizes. A mere ranking of functions would ignore the magnitude of differences between mean scores of different functions. Using LSD tests, we would be in a better position to identify the strategic functional significance mixes for firms pursuing different grand corporate strategies.

Since the LSD test can be and often is misused, statisticians caution against its indiscriminate use. In this study, in view of the nature of the data involved, a watered-down version of the LSD test will be used. The test used would not be a true or legitimate LSD test; it would only be an "approximate" LSD test since a set of means would be compared using the same technique but with a few assumptions. For one thing, in any data analysis repeated measures tend to cause some dependence; however, the usual LSD test assumes independence. Therefore, our assumption of independence would provide an "approximate" LSD test statistic. This approximation would make our LSD test more conservative in the sense that we would not be overstating the significance; that is, if the test shows no significance there might be some significance, but the test would not show significance when in fact there is none.

PROBLEMS AND LIMITATIONS

This study focuses primarily on top managers' perceptions of the relative importance of key result areas in different organizational functions to effective implementation of different grand corporate strategies. It seeks to identify critical or strategically significant function(s) for effective implementation of each type of grand corporate strategy. Therefore, the scope of this study is specific and limited. It does not purport to investigate the entire gamut of problems involved in the field of corporate strategy. It concentrates only on the problems of corporate strategy-implementation; and although it utilizes the functional tasks' influence-mix approach to corporate strategy, only the influence of organizational functions on corporate strategy implementation is examined. Their influence on the formulation and evaluation of corporate strategy is not in the purview of this study.

The field of business policy focuses on the total organization and deals with the problems and functions of top management. It is, therefore, apparent that any business-policy phenomenon involves a vast array of variables, most of which are difficult to isolate, define, and measure. Steiner and Miner (1977) point out, "The scope of managerial activities associated with implementation is virtually coextensive with the entire process of management" (pp. 607-8). In large corporations, according to Mintzberg (1977) "research shows that most work processes of senior managers are unstructured and that they require a profound integration of various aspects of the organization and its environment" (p. 93). The variables involved in the field of business policy are, therefore, not easily amenable to clear-cut, cause-and-effect relationships. Even when the independent and dependent variables are clearly isolated and defined, they are influenced by a vast array of mediating or intervening variables that cannot be ignored without making the study too simplistic or unrealistic; nor can they all be considered without making the study too unwieldy and infeasible. This study, therefore, examines the influence of six key mediating variables: size, corporate diversity, industry, production system, organizational structure, and perceived environmental uncertainty; it does not analyze the influence of all other possible mediating variables.

Another limitation of this cross-sectional study is that it addresses itself to the corporate strategies of large (the top 1,000) U.S. industrial corporations only, and therefore the conclusions derived from this study are not necessarily applicable to corporate strategies of firms in nonindustrial sectors, such as transportation, utilities, banking, and insurance. The findings may not also necessarily apply to smaller industrial firms (less than $100 million in annual sales).

However, the major limitation of this study is that it involves a static analysis of corporate strategy which is an inherently dynamic concept. The study, therefore, is not longitudinal in scope and nature. However, it is extremely important to bear in mind that for the same firm, even without a change in the grand corporate strategy, the same top manager may perceive the functional strategic significance mix differently at two different points in time.

Finally, the study's findings are based on senior executives' perceptions and opinions rather than on the actual observations of real world actions and results. Therefore, this study is marked by a total reliance on top-level executives for data gathering. There are various reasons why this reliance on top-level executives is essential and inevitable. Top management by its very nature is still very much an art, and this makes top-management planning a highly individualized process.

The "theory" of business policy is yet to evolve, although some contingency paradigms have been developed in recent times. In business policy, like in any other emerging discipline, sophisticated observation and description must precede normative prescription. There is a need in the business-policy literature for more rigorous, empirical studies of corporations and top executives, so that their collective wisdom can be effectively crystalized (by identifying patterns) into a systematized common body of knowledge that is useful for both theory and practice.

Another reason for reliance on top-level executives for data gathering is to be found in the nature of the field itself. The field of business policy focuses on the organization as a whole. Only people at the top have this overall, organizationwide perspective. Most successful top executives are said to have the "helicopter quality"— an ability to see problems from an overall perspective. Their responsibilities require that they have access to information about how the entire organization operates. Therefore, top-level executives (unlike divisional or functional managers) are the most knowledgeable people to provide reliable and meaningful information about their firm's overall operations and environments. This factor is equally important in case of managerial perceptions of their firm's environments. Unlike divisional or functional managers, the boundary-spanning role of top-level executives is not restricted or partial. As grand strategists, they are responsible for an on-going appraisal of the total environment and for formulating appropriate strategic responses for the accomplishment of corporate goals.

One final reason why the data for this study were gathered from top-level executives is that it was the only feasible way to obtain much of the required data. For variables like size, industry classification, or the predominant production system, the research investigator can obtain measures of these variables through personal observations or through data collected by independent and reliable secondary sources. Therefore, measurement of such variables does not pose any problem, and where respondents are asked, as a matter of convenience, to give such information about their organizations, its veracity can be easily verified by reference to the relevant secondary data. Such verification, of course, was not possible in this study, since the respondents had a choice to remain anonymous (without which most top-level executives would have been reluctant to give any information about their companies), making data collection (and, therefore, the entire study) an almost impossible task.

However, variables like the grand corporate strategy currently pursued by the firm can only be measured by the top-level executives of the firm itself. If the research investigator were to do this himself, he would have to spend an inordinate amount of time going through the various company records and talking to different top managers, assuming of course that he is allowed an access to these sources by all the firms in his study sample, which would of necessity be very small. Clearly, this has to be ruled out. Second, available published data also cannot be used for this purpose. Most published data relate to past performance rather than the current grand strategy of the firm.

NOTE

1. For an extended discussion of least significant difference (LSD) tests, see Robert G. D. Steel and James H. Torrie, Principles and Procedures of Statistics (New York: McGraw-Hill, 1960), pp. 106-7; George W. Snedecor and William G. Cochran, Statistical Methods, 6th ed. (Ames: Iowa State University Press, 1973), pp. 271-75; and Lee H. Smith and Donald R. William, Statistical Analysis for Business Decisions: A Conceptual Approach (Belmont, Calif.: Wadsworth, 1971), pp. 462-68.

6

ANALYSES
OF DATA

Having set forth the nature of this study's research methodology in the previous chapter, this chapter deals with the analyses of data relevant to the research questions delineated in Chapters 4 and 5. Additional analyses of data not directly related to the research questions raised in this study are also presented. The significance and implications of the results will be discussed in Chapter 7.

RESEARCH QUESTION 1

Research Question 1: Is the relative strategic significance of the seven organizational functions different for firms pursuing varying grand corporate strategies?

For this research question, the study's sample of 249 firms was categorized by grand corporate strategy, and for each category the seven organizational functions were ranked by their mean strategic significance scores. Results of the slippage test (Conover 1971) showed T = 5 (p < .02). This suggests that the functional significance scores were distributed differently in separate grand corporate strategy groupings. As shown in Table 6.1, general administration was the top-ranked function for the overall sample, followed by finance and then a group of personnel, marketing, and public and government relations. The top three functions in each of the four classes of grand corporate strategy were different from those in the overall sample. Only general administration was consistently ranked among the top several functions in each type.

For firms pursuing stability strategy, the paired t-tests resulted in overlapping paired differences with the result that no function(s)

TABLE 6.1

Mean Strategic Significance Scores by Grand Corporate Strategy

Grand Corporate Strategy									
Stability (N = 29)		Internal Growth (N = 104)		External Acquisitive Growth (N = 96)		Retrenchment (N = 20)		All Firms (N = 249)	
GADM	4.97	GADM	5.02	MKTG	4.71	MKTG	4.56	GADM	4.79
PGR	4.94	FIN	4.75	GADM	4.66	FIN	4.06	FIN	4.64
PERS	4.72	PERS	4.75	FIN	4.62	PERS	4.03	PERS	4.48
FIN	4.70	ERD	4.69	PERS	4.22	GADM	3.93	MKTG	4.47
ERD	4.52	PGR	4.68	PGR	4.21	PGR	3.67	PGR	4.44
PROD	4.44	MKTG	4.28	ERD	3.93	PROD	3.50	ERD	4.28
MKTG	4.31	PROD	4.19	PROD	3.84	ERD	3.48	PROD	4.03
F = 1.99		F = 9.06[b]		F = 21.76[b]		F = 4.46[b]		F = 17.41[b]	

[a]Significant at $p < .05$ level.
[b]Significant at $p < .01$ level.

Note: LSD test between means statistically significant at $p < .05$ level.

Source: Compiled by the authors.

113

emerged as having a mean score(s) significantly different from the rest.

For firms pursuing an internal growth strategy, the mean scores of marketing and production were found to be significantly different (lower) from the mean scores of all the other functions. Thus, for firms pursuing internal growth strategy, these functions were found to have the lowest strategic significance.

For firms pursuing an external acquisitive growth strategy, there was no significant difference between the mean scores of the three top-ranked functions, marketing, general administration, and finance. However, their mean scores were significantly different from the mean scores of the remaining five functions.

For firms pursuing a retrenchment strategy, the mean score of marketing was found to be significantly different from the mean scores of all other functions. Thus, for such firms marketing was found to have the highest strategic significance.

For all firms considered together, the mean strategic significance score of general administration was found to be significantly different from the mean scores of all the other functions. The mean score of finance was second; personnel, marketing, and public and government relations, as a group, ranked third. The mean score of the last-ranked function (production) was significantly different from the six higher-ranked functions, and engineering and R&D was the second-lowest-ranked function. Thus, for all industrial firms general administration was found to have the highest strategic significance. Next in importance were finance, personnel, marketing, and public and government relations. Of all seven functions, production was found to have the lowest strategic significance; engineering and R&D was the second lowest.

In addition to the approximate least significant difference (LSD) tests for each cell in Table 6.1, an F-ratio was also calculated from an analysis of variance (one-way classification by organizational function) for the strategic significance score (grand mean) in each cell. The F-ratios shown in Table 6.1 were calculated on the assumption that the mean strategic significance scores of each of the seven organizational functions came from seven independent samples rather than from the same sample (a repeated-measures design); thus, it was assumed that the mean scores in each cell were independent. This necessitated a change in the degrees of freedom from the calculated F-ratios for ascertaining the critical values. Thus, in a repeated-measures analysis of variance (AOV) test, our assumption of independence yields critical values for F-ratios that are approximate but conservative, in the sense that significance is never likely to be overstated.

Table 6.1 indicates that F-ratios are significant (at $p < .05$ level) for all cells except cell 1 (stability strategy). For firms pur-

TABLE 6.2

Calculated F-Ratios from One-way Analysis of Variance for the Mean Strategic Significance Scores of Each of the Seven Different Organizational Functions

(N = 249)

Organizational Function	AOV I $(F_{3,245})$	AOV II $(F_{2,246})$	AOV III $(F_{3,245})$	AOV IV $(F_{3,245})$	AOV V $(F_{2,246})$	AOV VI $(F_{4,244})$	AOV VII $(F_{1,247})$
GADM	17.02[a]	0.56	0.98	2.20	3.18[b]	0.40	0.18
PROD	7.74[a]	1.17	0.35	5.01[a]	1.62	0.45	2.21
ERD	14.58[a]	6.21[a]	2.74[b]	0.83	4.96[a]	2.59[b]	0.11
MKTG	3.90[a]	0.34	0.21	5.01[a]	4.09[b]	0.95	6.73[a]
FIN	9.76[a]	5.17[a]	1.90	0.75	1.14	2.73[b]	0.59
PERS	18.28[a]	0.43	0.62	0.37	2.38	0.71	1.50
PGR	8.20[a]	12.38[a]	2.79[b]	1.22	4.94[a]	1.33	0.53

AOV I   = one-way classification by grand corporate strategy
AOV II   = one-way classification by firm size
AOV III   = one-way classification by corporate diversity
AOV IV   = one-way classification by industry
AOV V   = one-way classification by production system
AOV VI   = one-way classification by organizational structure
AOV VII   = one-way classification by perceived environmental uncertainty

[a] Significant at p < .01 level.
[b] Significant at p < .05 level.

Source: Compiled by the authors.

suing a stability strategy, the mean scores of the seven functions were not significantly different. For firms pursuing the other three grand corporate strategies and also for all the firms in the sample (N = 249), the mean scores of the seven functions were significantly different (at $p < .05$ level). These F-ratios, therefore, indicate the magnitude of differences between mean scores of different functions in each cell.

Finally, as shown in Table 6.2 (column AOV I), an analysis of variance (one-way classification by grand corporate strategy) for the mean strategic significance scores of each of the seven different organizational functions indicated significant differences (at $p < .01$ level). In fact, the actual critical value for the F-ratio of each function (except marketing) was $p < .005$, indicating highly significant differences. The data presented in Table 6.2 clearly indicate that significant differences do exist among the mean strategic significance scores of each function attributable to the grand corporate strategies.

Thus, the results of these analyses provide evidence that the strategic significance of each organizational function is not the same for the four types of grand corporate strategies.

RESEARCH QUESTION 2

Research Question 2: For firms pursuing a particular grand corporate strategy, is the relative strategic significance of the seven organizational functions different for firms of varying size?

For this research question, the study's sample of 249 firms was categorized into 12 cells by means of a 3×4 factorial design of firm size $\times$ grand corporate strategy. As shown in Table 6.3, within each of the 12 cells and the overall column and row cells, the seven organizational functions were ranked by their mean strategic significance scores.

The results of approximate LSD tests showed significant differences in mean values for only three cells. For large firms with internal growth strategies, the lowest-ranked production and marketing had mean scores significantly different from those of the five higher-ranked functions. For medium-sized firms with external acquisitive growth strategies, the mean scores of top-ranked general administration and marketing were found to be significantly different from the mean scores of the other five functions; third-ranked finance had a mean score significantly different from the rest. For large firms with external acquisitive growth strategies, the cellar function production had a mean score significantly different from all the other higher-ranked functions.

TABLE 6.3

Rankings of the Seven Organizational Functions by Their Mean Strategic Significance Scores within Each of the 12 Cells in a 3 × 4 Factorial Design of Firm Size × Grand Corporate Strategy

Firm Size		Grand Corporate Strategy								Overall Row Means	
		Stability		Internal Growth		External Acquisitive Growth		Retrenchment			
Small		N_{11} = 5		N_{12} = 24		N_{13} = 22		N_{14} = 9		R_1 = 60	
		GADM	4.40	GADM	5.14	MKTG	4.52	MKTG	4.31	GADM	4.71
		FIN	4.13	PERS	4.89	GADM	4.52	PERS	4.22	MKTG	4.49
		PERS	3.86	FIN	4.86	FIN	4.31	GADM	4.18	PERS	4.44
		PROD	3.76	ERD	4.80	PERS	4.16	PROD	3.86	FIN	4.41
		MKTG	3.40	MKTG	4.76	PROD	3.91	FIN	3.62	PROD	4.13
		ERD	3.24	PROD	4.51	ERD	3.74	PGR	3.17	ERD	4.03
		PGR	2.95	PGR	4.19	PGR	3.72	ERD	3.11	PGR	3.76
										F = 5.57[a]	
Medium		N_{21} = 9		N_{22} = 35		N_{23} = 34		N_{24} = 6		R_2 = 84	
		GADM	5.28	GADM	4.87	GADM	4.75	MKTG	4.75	GADM	4.79
		PERS	5.27	PERS	4.77	MKTG	4.70	ERD	3.93	PERS	4.43
		PGR	5.11	FIN	4.57	FIN	4.30	FIN	3.91	FIN	4.41
		PROD	4.96	PGR	4.42	PERS	4.00	GADM	3.82	MKTG	4.40
		ERD	4.69	ERD	4.29	PGR	3.95	PERS	3.60	PGR	4.23
		FIN	4.55	MKTG	4.01	ERD	3.83	PGR	3.42	ERD	4.12
		MKTG	4.54	PROD	3.87	PROD	3.81	PROD	3.27	PROD	3.92
										F = 8.11[b]	
Large		N_{31} = 15		N_{32} = 45		N_{33} = 40		N_{34} = 5		R_3 = 105	
		PGR	5.03	GADM	5.06	MKTG	4.81	MKTG	4.78	GADM	4.83
		GADM	4.98	ERD	4.95	GADM	4.67	FIN	3.96	FIN	4.74
		FIN	4.88	FIN	4.87	FIN	4.65	PGR	3.95	PGR	4.62
		ERD	4.85	PERS	4.84	PGR	4.40	PERS	3.94	ERD	4.55
		PERS	4.72	PGR	4.74	PERS	4.19	ERD	3.68	PERS	4.53
		MKTG	4.48	PROD	4.26	ERD	4.11	GADM	3.64	MKTG	4.51
		PROD	4.35	MKTG	4.23	PROD	3.84	PROD	3.14	PROD	4.06
										F = 9.14[b]	
Total		N = 29		N = 104		N = 96		N = 20		N = 249	

[a]Significant at $p < .05$ level.
[b]Significant at $p < .01$ level.

Note: LSD between means statistically significant at $p < .05$ level.

Source: Compiled by the authors.

TABLE 6.4

Calculated F-Ratios from Unweighted Analysis of Variance for the Mean Strategic Significance Scores of Each of the Seven Different Organizational Functions in Each of the Six Different Factorial Designs Used in Data Analyses

	Organizational Function						
	GADM	PROD	ERD	MKTG	FIN	PERS	PGR
I. 4 × 3 Factorial design of grand corporate strategy × firm size							
Effect of GCS ($F_{3,237}$)	20.82^a	8.97^a	8.38^a	2.62^b	9.10^a	10.76^a	5.95^a
Effect of size ($F_{2,237}$)	0.42	0.22	5.88^a	1.66	2.68	0.48	12.11^a
Interaction effect ($F_{6,237}$)	2.58^b	3.41^a	2.64^b	2.46^b	0.68	3.94^a	2.73^b
II. 4 × 4 Factorial design of grand corporate strategy × corporate diversity							
Effect of GCS ($F_{3,233}$)	17.07^a	7.74^a	8.41^a	1.40	10.24^a	11.59^a	8.69^a
Effect of corporate diversity ($F_{3,233}$)	0.27	0.15	2.09	0.69	1.46	0.57	2.69^b
Interaction effect ($F_{9,233}$)	0.76	0.59	2.64^a	1.01	0.68	0.97	3.88^a
III. 4 × 4 Factorial design of grand corporate strategy × industry							
Effect of GCS ($F_{3,233}$)	17.91^a	11.36^a	10.75^a	1.02	11.10^a	12.35^a	10.59^a
Effect of industry ($F_{3,233}$)	2.29	4.54^a	2.27	3.08^b	0.21	0.29	1.91
Interaction effect ($F_{9,233}$)	1.94^b	1.36	0.46	0.44	0.78	1.38	1.38
IV. 4 × 3 Factorial design of grand corporate strategy × production system							
Effect of GCS ($F_{3,236}$)	17.37^a	7.65^a	15.02^a	4.61^a	4.01^a	10.37^b	9.09^a
Effect of production system ($F_{2,236}$)	3.06^b	1.98	4.08^b	6.18^a	0.99	2.24	2.97
Interaction effect ($F_{6,236}$)	1.45	1.26	1.26	2.11	0.36	0.74	0.86
V. 4 × 5 Factorial design of grand corporate strategy × organizational structure							
Effect of GCS ($F_{3,229}$)	18.27^a	8.41^a	4.39^a	1.28	8.12^a	10.36^a	5.56^a
Effect of organizational structure ($F_{4,229}$)	0.83	0.80	1.44	0.74	1.65	1.17	1.53
Interaction effect ($F_{12,229}$)	1.74	0.54	1.46	0.46	1.92^b	3.16^a	2.88^a
VI. 4 × 3 Factorial design of grand corporate strategy × perceived environmental uncertainty							
Effect of GCS ($F_{3,236}$)	16.53^a	7.58^a	14.74^a	4.53^a	4.08^a	10.98^b	9.60^a
Effect of PEU ($F_{2,236}$)	0.47	1.50	0.99	6.92^a	0.68	3.29^b	1.72
Interaction effect ($F_{6,236}$)	0.29	1.02	1.50	1.13	1.19	2.81^b	3.60^a

[a] Significant at p < .01 level.
[b] Significant at p < .05 level.

Source: Compiled by the authors.

However, the same tests showed significant differences for the overall row means. For both small and medium-sized firms, top-ranked general administration had mean scores significantly different from all other functions; marketing, personnel, and finance had mean scores that were not significantly different from one another, but were significantly different from those of the four other functions. In large firms lowest-ranked production had a mean score significantly different from all the other higher-ranked functions.

The F-ratios for all three size groups were significant at $p < .05$ level (see Table 6.3). Thus, the mean scores of the seven functions varied in each size group.

However, the F-ratios from one-way analysis of variance by size for the mean strategic significance score of each function showed significance (at $p < .01$ level) for only three functions: engineering and R&D, finance, and public and government relations (see Table 6.2). Thus, it appears that there do exist significant differences among the mean strategic significance scores of each of these three functions attributable to firm size. On the other hand, the strategic significance of general administration, production-operations, marketing, and personnel appears not to vary across the three size categories.

An unweighted AOV for the mean strategic significance score of each function in the factorial design shown in Table 6.4, showed significance (at $p < .01$ level) for only two functions—engineering and R&D and public and government relations—when the effect of size was considered. The effect of size on finance was found to be significant at only $p < .1$ level. The results of these unweighted factorial AOVs in so far as they relate to the effect of size corroborate the results of one-way AOVs by size discussed in the preceding paragraph. F-ratios for the effect of grand corporate strategy showed significance (at $p < .05$ level) for all the seven functions. Similarly, the F-ratios for the interaction effect of size and grand corporate strategy were also significant (at $p < .05$ level) for all functions except finance $(F = 0.68, p > .5)$.

To sum up, the results seem to indicate that when the effects of firm size and grand corporate strategy are considered, with the exception of finance, there do exist significant differences among the mean strategic significance scores of each function. The strategic significance of finance, on the other hand, does not seem to differ in industrial firms when the interacting effects of size and grand corporate strategy are considered.

TABLE 6.5

Rankings of the Seven Organizational Functions by Their Mean Strategic Significance Scores within Each of the 16 Cells in a 4 × 4 Factorial Design of Corporate Diversity × Grand Corporate Strategy

Corporate Diversity	Grand Corporate Strategy				Overall Row Means
	Stability	Internal Growth	External Acquisitive Growth	Retrenchment	
Single business	$N_{11} = 5$	$N_{12} = 10$	$N_{13} = 8$	$N_{14} = 5$	$R_1 = 28$
	PGR 5.30	GADM 5.26	GADM 4.35	MKTG 4.73	GADM 4.74
	GADM 5.00	FIN 5.02	MKTG 4.17	PERS 4.43	PERS 4.57
	PERS 5.00	PERS 5.01	FIN 4.07	GADM 4.06	FIN 4.47
	MKTG 4.63	PGR 4.98	PERS 3.82	FIN 3.95	PGR 4.37
	PROD 4.54	PROD 4.25	ERD 3.75	PGR 3.85	MKTG 4.34
	FIN 4.53	MKTG 4.15	PROD 3.75	PROD 3.76	PROD 4.07
	ERD 4.12	ERD 3.86	PGR 3.34	ERD 3.40	ERD 3.79
					F = 1.83
Dominant business	$N_{21} = 5$	$N_{22} = 20$	$N_{23} = 25$	$N_{24} = 5$	$R_2 = 55$
	ERD 5.00	PERS 4.90	MKTG 4.77	MKTG 3.98	GADM 4.65
	PERS 4.86	GADM 4.86	GADM 4.62	GADM 3.86	MKTG 4.46
	GADM 4.82	ERD 4.76	FIN 4.21	PERS 3.63	PERS 4.38
	PGR 4.75	FIN 4.72	PERS 4.02	PROD 3.46	FIN 4.35
	PROD 4.70	PGR 4.46	PGR 4.00	FIN 3.42	ERD 4.19
	FIN 4.47	MKTG 4.31	ERD 3.90	ERD 2.52	PGR 4.09
	MKTG 4.05	PROD 4.12	PROD 3.73	PGR 2.45	PROD 3.93
					F = 4.06

120

Related business	$N_{31} = 14$		$N_{32} = 54$		$N_{33} = 42$		$N_{34} = 6$		$R_3 = 116$	
	GADM	5.11	GADM	5.04	MKTG	4.71	MKTG	4.92	GADM	4.85
	PGR	5.07	PERS	4.80	GADM	4.68	ERD	3.97	FIN	4.60
	ERD	4.79	ERD	4.70	FIN	4.60	GADM	3.73	PERS	4.53
	FIN	4.75	FIN	4.68	PGR	4.33	PERS	3.69	MKTG	4.50
	PERS	4.71	PGR	4.53	PERS	4.24	FIN	3.64	PGR	4.47
	PROD	4.47	MKTG	4.30	ERD	3.98	PGR	3.54	ERD	4.41
	MKTG	4.46	PROD	4.10	PROD	3.90	PROD	3.32	PROD	4.03 [a]
									F	= 9.35 [a]

Unrelated business	$N_{41} = 5$		$N_{42} = 20$		$N_{43} = 21$		$N_{44} = 4$		$R_4 = 50$	
	GADM	4.70	ERD	5.03	MKTG	4.83	MKTG	4.53	GADM	4.81
	FIN	4.64	GADM	4.97	GADM	4.80	FIN	4.30	FIN	4.69
	PERS	4.46	FIN	4.94	FIN	4.55	PERS	4.21	MKTG	4.48
	PROD	3.98	PERS	4.74	PERS	4.10	GADM	4.18	PERS	4.40
	MKTG	3.85	PROD	4.47	PGR	3.99	ERD	4.15	ERD	4.36
	ERD	3.72	PGR	4.26	ERD	3.90	PGR	4.00	PROD	4.10
	PGR	3.00	MKTG	4.26	PROD	3.90	PROD	3.50	PGR	4.00 [b]
									F	= 5.62 [b]

Total	$N = 29$	$N = 104$	$N = 96$	$N = 20$	$N = 249$

[a]Significant at $p < .01$ level.
[b]Significant at $p < .05$ level.

Note: LSD test between means statistically significant at $p < .05$ level.

Source: Compiled by the authors.

121

RESEARCH QUESTION 3

Research Question 3: For firms pursuing a particular grand corporate strategy, is the relative strategic significance of the seven organizational functions different for firms with varying degrees of corporate diversity?

For this research question, the study's sample of 249 firms was categorized into 16 cells by means of a 4×4 factorial design of corporate diversity $\times$ grand corporate strategy. As shown in Table 6.5, within each of the 16 cells and the overall column and row cells the seven organizational functions were ranked by their mean strategic significance scores.

The results of approximate LSD tests showed significant differences in mean scores for only seven cells. General administration's mean score was significantly higher than all other functions for the related business firms with an internal growth strategy. For the dominant business firms with an external growth strategy, the mean scores of top-ranked marketing and general administration were significantly different from the mean scores of the other five functions. The mean scores of the top three functions—marketing, general administration, and finance—were significantly different from those of the remaining four functions in the case of both related and unrelated business firms with an external growth strategy. In the case of all the related business firms, top-ranked general administration and lowest-ranked production had mean scores significantly different from all other functions.

F-ratios for the repeated-measures AOVs for the four diversity groups showed significance (at $p < .05$ level) only in the case of the related and unrelated business firms. Thus, the mean scores of the seven functions in these two categories were significantly different. Conversely, the mean scores of the seven functions in the case of the single dominant business firms were not significantly different.

As shown in Table 6.2, the F-ratios from the AOV (one-way) classification by corporate diversity for the mean strategic significance score of each function showed significance (at $p < .05$ level) for only two functions: engineering and R&D and public and government relations. The F-ratios for the effect of corporate diversity in an unweighted AOV for a 4×4 factorial design of strategy $\times$ diversity (Table 6.4) showed significance (at $p < .05$ level) only in the case of public and government relations. However, the effect of grand corporate strategy was significant for all functions except marketing. The F-ratios for the interaction effect of grand corporate strategy and corporate diversity showed significance only in the case of engineering and R&D and public and government relations. F-ratios for marketing showed no significant effects of strategy, corporate diversity, or their interaction.

The results of the analyses by grand corporate strategy and corporate diversity indicate that significant differences do exist among the mean strategic significance scores of marketing attributable to grand corporate strategy and/or corporate diversity. Conversely, for public and government relations, there do exist significant differences among their respective mean scores attributable to grand corporate strategy and/or corporate diversity. For general administration, production/operations, finance, and personnel the effect of corporate diversity and the interaction effect of strategy and diversity do not seem to show any differences among these functions' mean strategic significance scores.

RESEARCH QUESTION 4

Research Question 4: For firms pursuing a particular grand corporate strategy, is the relative strategic significance of the seven organizational functions different for firms in varying industries?

For this research question, the study's sample of 249 firms was categorized into 16 cells by means of a 4×4 factorial design of industry $\times$ grand corporate strategy. As shown in Table 6.6, within each of the 16 cells and the overall column and row cells the seven organizational functions were ranked by their mean strategic significance scores.

The results of approximate LSD tests showed significant differences in the mean scores only in a few cases. In the case of firms with stability and retrenchment strategies, the sample size in some cells was less than five. For firms in the capital goods industry with a stability strategy, the mean scores of the top four functions were significantly different from the mean scores of the bottom three functions. The mean scores of marketing, general administration, and finance were significantly different from the mean scores of the last four functions in both the capital and producer goods industries for firms with an external acquisitive growth strategy. Production had significantly lower scores than all other functions in both the consumer nondurable and producer goods industries. General administration, on the other hand, had significantly higher scores than all the other functions in both the capital and producer goods industries.

The F-ratios for the repeated-measures AOVs for each of the four industry groups showed significance (at $p < .05$ level) in the case of the consumer nondurable, capital, and producer goods industries. Thus, the mean scores of the seven functions in these three industries were significantly different. On the other hand, the mean scores of the seven functions in the case of the consumer durable goods industries were not significantly different.

The results of one-way AOVs by industry (Table 6.2) and unweighted AOVs of the factorial design of grand corporate strategy $\times$

TABLE 6.6

Rankings of the Seven Organizational Functions by Their Mean Strategic Significance Scores within Each of the 16 Cells in a 4 × 4 Factorial Design of Industry × Grand Corporate Strategy

Consumer nondurable goods

	Grand Corporate Strategy				Overall Row Means
	Stability $N_{11} = 10$	Internal Growth $N_{12} = 32$	External Acquisitive Growth $N_{13} = 25$	Retrenchment $N_{14} = 6$	$R_1 = 73$
	GADM 4.77	GADM 5.11	MKTG 4.54	MKTG 4.60	GADM 4.70
	PGR 4.58	FIN 4.92	GADM 4.41	PERS 4.24	FIN 4.53
	FIN 4.51	PERS 4.89	FIN 4.23	PGR 3.88	PGR 4.48
	ERD 4.50	PGR 4.84	PGR 4.12	FIN 3.77	MKTG 4.45
	MKTG 4.29	ERD 4.68	PERS 3.95	GADM 3.60	PERS 4.43
	PERS 4.29	MKTG 4.40	ERD 3.77	PROD 3.33	ERD 4.21
	PROD 3.91	PROD 4.11	PROD 3.41	ERD 3.10	PROD 3.78
					$F = 7.35$[a]

Consumer durable goods

	Grand Corporate Strategy				Overall Row Means
	Stability $N_{21} = 4$	Internal Growth $N_{22} = 10$	External Acquisitive Growth $N_{23} = 14$	Retrenchment $N_{24} = 6$	$R_2 = 34$
	PERS 5.50	ERD 4.94	MKTG 4.79	MKTG 4.88	MKTG 4.76
	GADM 5.48	GADM 4.66	GADM 4.68	ERD 4.07	GADM 4.60
	PROD 5.38	MKTG 4.64	FIN 4.24	PGR 4.04	ERD 4.49
	FIN 5.23	PERS 4.60	ERD 4.19	PERS 3.88	FIN 4.38
	ERD 5.10	FIN 4.55	PERS 4.09	FIN 3.88	PERS 4.37
	MKTG 4.88	PGR 4.53	PROD 4.07	GADM 3.73	PGR 4.24
	PGR 4.75	PROD 4.52	PGR 3.98	PROD 3.23	PROD 4.21
					$F = 1.58$

Industry

Capital goods

$N_{31} = 4$		$N_{32} = 28$		$N_{33} = 24$		$N_{34} = 5$		$R_3 = 61$	
GADM	5.33	GADM	5.19	MKTG	4.88	MKTG	4.45	GADM	4.95
PROD	4.85	ERD	4.92	GADM	4.77	GADM	4.18	MKTG	4.70
PERS	4.82	FIN	4.84	FIN	4.58	PERS	3.86	FIN	4.64
FIN	4.68	PERS	4.83	PERS	4.20	PROD	3.84	PERS	4.50
MKTG	4.38	MKTG	4.64	PROD	4.19	FIN	3.76	ERD	4.36
PGR	4.13	PROD	4.42	PGR	4.13	ERD	3.32	PROD	4.31
ERD	4.05	PGR	4.37	ERD	3.98	PGR	2.80	PGR	4.13
								$F = 5.11$[b]	

Producer goods

$N_{41} = 11$		$N_{42} = 34$		$N_{43} = 33$		$N_{44} = 3$		$R_4 = 81$	
PGR	5.00	GADM	4.89	GADM	4.76	GADM	4.60	GADM	4.82
PERS	4.86	PERS	4.83	MKTG	4.67	MKTG	4.00	FIN	4.56
GADM	4.85	FIN	4.63	FIN	4.59	PROD	3.80	PERS	4.53
FIN	4.55	ERD	4.44	PERS	4.19	PERS	3.76	PGR	4.23
ERD	4.51	PGR	4.30	PGR	4.07	FIN	3.70	ERD	4.19
PROD	4.43	PROD	3.96	ERD	3.90	ERD	3.47	MKTG	4.19
MKTG	4.10	MKTG	3.76	PROD	3.82	PGR	2.42	PROD	3.96
								$F = 9.21$[a]	

Total

$N = 29$	$N = 104$	$N = 96$	$N = 20$	$N = 249$

[a]Significant at $p < .01$ level.
[b]Significant at $p < .05$ level.

Note: LSD test between means statistically significant at $p < .05$ level.

Source: Compiled by the authors.

125

industry (Table 6.4) for the mean strategic significance score of each function showed significance for the effect of industry for only two functions: production-operations and marketing. Thus, it appears that, barring these two functions, there do not exist significant differences in the mean strategic significance scores of different functions. The effect of grand corporate strategy (main effect) was found to be significant for all functions except marketing, whereas the interaction effect was significant only for general administration.

The results of these AOVs seem to indicate significant differences among the mean scores of production-operations, marketing, and general administration attributable to grand corporate strategy and/or industry. For engineering and R&D, finance, personnel, and public and government relations, the effect of industry types and the interaction effect of industry and strategy do not seem to show any differences among these functions' mean strategic significance scores.

RESEARCH QUESTION 5

Research Question 5: For firms pursuing a particular grand corporate strategy, is the relative strategic significance of the seven organizational functions different for firms with varying production systems?

For this research question, the study's sample of 249 firms was categorized into 12 cells by means of a 3×4 factorial design of production system × grand corporate strategy, together with three cells for all firms for each type of production system. As shown in Table 6.7, within each cell the seven organizational functions have been ranked according to their mean strategic significance scores.

The results of approximate LSD tests revealed significant differences in the mean scores of different functions for only four cells. For firms with an internal growth strategy, general administration had a mean score significantly higher—production, significantly lower—than all other functions in the case of the large-batch and mass production. Marketing had a mean score significantly lower than all the functions in the case of the continuous-process production. For firms with an external growth strategy, marketing, general administration, and finance had mean scores significantly higher than the rest for the large-batch-and-mass-production and continuous-process firms. Engineering and R&D and production had mean scores significantly lower than other functions for continuous-process production firms. General administration had a significantly higher mean score than all other functions for firms with both the small-batch and mass-production systems. Additionally, for firms with the mass-production

TABLE 6.7

Mean Functional Importance Scores of Organizational Functions: Grand Strategy by Production System

Grand Corporate Strategy

Unit and small batch

Stability	Internal Growth	External Acquisitive Growth	Retrenchment	All Firms
N = 4	N = 17	N = 14	N = 6	N = 41
GADM 5.33	GADM 4.76	GADM 4.96	MKTG 4.29	GADM 4.80
PERS 4.90	ERD 4.58	FIN 4.64	GADM 4.18	FIN 4.50
PROD 4.85	FIN 4.45	MKTG 4.59	FIN 4.14	MKTG 4.41
FIN 4.68	MKTG 4.32	ERD 4.40	PERS 3.90	PERS 4.26
PGR 4.41	PERS 4.29	PGR 4.21	PROD 3.80	ERD 4.25
MKTG 4.38	PGR 4.10	PERS 4.20	PGR 3.11	PROD 4.12
ERD 4.05	PROD 4.02	PROD 4.16	ERD 3.10	PGR 4.02
				F = 2.66[a]

Large batch and mass production

Stability	Internal Growth	External Acquisitive Growth	Retrenchment	All Firms
N = 13	N = 66	N = 69	N = 9	N = 137
GADM 4.93	GADM 5.14	MKTG 4.84	MKTG 4.67	GADM 4.88
PGR 4.92	PERS 4.87	GADM 4.70	FIN 4.14	FIN 4.72
PERS 4.78	ERD 4.85	FIN 4.68	PERS 4.00	MKTG 4.62
FIN 4.75	FIN 4.81	PERS 4.29	PGR 3.89	PERS 4.60
ERD 4.62	PGR 4.74	PGR 4.27	GADM 3.84	PGR 4.54
MKTG 4.29	MKTG 4.52	ERD 4.02	ERD 3.75	ERD 4.46
PROD 4.28	PROD 4.28	PROD 3.95	PROD 3.23	PROD 4.09
				F = 10.22[b]

Continuous process

Stability	Internal Growth	External Acquisitive Growth	Retrenchment	All Firms
N = 12	N = 21	N = 32	N = 5	N = 70
PGR 5.14	PGR 4.95	MKTG 4.62	MKTG 4.68	GADM 4.61
GADM 4.90	GADM 4.84	FIN 4.51	PERS 4.24	FIN 4.56
FIN 4.65	FIN 4.77	GADM 4.48	PGR 3.93	PGR 4.51
PERS 4.60	PERS 4.73	PERS 4.13	FIN 3.82	PERS 4.40
ERD 4.58	ERD 4.28	PGR 4.07	GADM 3.80	MKTG 4.23
PROD 4.47	PROD 4.03	ERD 3.61	PROD 3.62	ERD 3.96
MKTG 4.31	MKTG 3.47	PROD 3.58	ERD 3.44	PROD 3.87
				F = 7.81[b]

Total

Stability	Internal Growth	External Acquisitive Growth	Retrenchment	All Firms
N = 29	N = 104	N = 95	N = 20	N = 248

[a]p < .05.
[b]p < .01.

Note: LSD test between means statistically significant at p < .05.

Source: Compiled by the authors.

TABLE 6.8

Rankings of the Seven Organizational Functions by Their Mean Strategic Significance Scores within Each of the 20 Cells in a 5 × 4 Factorial Design of Organizational Structure × Grand Corporate Strategy

Organizational Structure	Stability	Internal Growth	External Acquisitive Growth	Retrenchment	Overall Row Means
Functional	$N_{11} = 6$	$N_{12} = 7$	$N_{13} = 8$	$N_{14} = 7$	$R_1 = 28$
	GADM 4.65	GADM 5.51	GADM 4.28	PERS 4.39	GADM 4.67
	PGR 4.50	FIN 5.35	MKTG 4.18	MKTG 4.34	PERS 4.40
	PERS 4.26	PERS 5.29	FIN 3.94	GADM 4.29	MKTG 4.24
	PROD 4.23	PGR 5.04	PERS 3.73	PROD 3.94	FIN 4.17
	ERD 4.17	ERD 4.57	PROD 3.64	FIN 3.61	PROD 4.05
	MKTG 4.02	PROD 4.47	ERD 3.43	PGR 3.25	PGR 3.91
	FIN 3.76	MKTG 4.41	PGR 3.06	ERD 3.09	ERD 3.79
					F = 1.94
Functional with one or more divisions or subsidiaries	$N_{21} = 11$	$N_{22} = 21$	$N_{23} = 19$	$N_{24} = 6$	$R_2 = 57$
	GADM 5.35	GADM 4.78	GADM 4.82	MKTG 4.58	GADM 4.78
	PGR 5.20	PERS 4.71	MKTG 4.65	FIN 3.76	PERS 4.52
	PERS 5.13	ERD 4.48	FIN 4.45	GADM 3.58	FIN 4.45
	FIN 5.03	PGR 4.37	PGR 4.30	ERD 3.57	MKTG 4.41
	ERD 4.91	FIN 4.34	PERS 4.26	PERS 3.55	PGR 4.40
	PROD 4.68	PROD 4.07	ERD 4.13	PGR 3.33	ERD 4.35
	MKTG 4.59	MKTG 4.04	PROD 3.98	PROD 3.25	PROD 4.07
					F = 2.98
Product division	$N_{31} = 8$	$N_{32} = 56$	$N_{33} = 44$	$N_{34} = 3$	$R_3 = 111$
	ERD 4.68	GADM 4.98	GADM 4.74	MKTG 4.71	GADM 4.82
	GADM 4.54	FIN 4.81	MKTG 4.72	PGR 3.67	FIN 4.69
	PGR 4.53	ERD 4.80	FIN 4.66	GADM 3.57	MKTG 4.48

FIN 4.52	PERS 4.75	PERS 4.19	FIN 3.45	PERS 4.47
PERS 4.48	PGR 4.36	PGR 4.14	PERS 3.29	ERD 4.43
PROD 4.14	MKTG 4.32	ERD 3.99	ERD 3.13	PGR 4.26
MKTG 4.09	PROD 4.10	PROD 3.88	PROD 2.87	PROD 3.98
				$F = 11.57$ [a]

Geographic division

$N_{41}=2$	$N_{42}=14$	$N_{43}=14$	$N_{44}=2$	$R_4=32$
FIN 5.05	PERS 5.30	MKTG 4.89	ERD 4.70	GADM 4.86
GADM 4.95	PGR 5.27	GADM 4.57	MKTG 4.63	PERS 4.63
PROD 4.80	GADM 5.20	PGR 4.27	FIN 4.41	MKTG 4.61
ERD 4.40	FIN 4.97	FIN 4.21	GADM 4.40	FIN 4.61
PERS 4.00	ERD 4.70	PERS 4.12	PERS 4.07	PGR 4.52
MKTG 3.88	MKTG 4.44	PROD 3.91	PROD 3.65	ERD 4.31
PGR 2.88	PROD 4.42	ERD 3.86	PGR 2.63	PROD 4.18
				$F = 1.6$

Holding company

$N_{51}=2$	$N_{52}=8$	$N_{53}=11$	$N_{54}=2$	$R_5=21$
PERS 5.86	GADM 5.12	MKTG 4.88	MKTG 4.94	GADM 4.70
GADM 5.60	FIN 4.68	GADM 4.45	PGR 4.88	MKTG 4.69
FIN 5.27	ERD 4.53	FIN 4.23	PERS 4.61	FIN 4.48
PGR 5.00	PROD 4.52	PGR 4.00	FIN 4.41	PERS 4.25
MKTG 4.94	PERS 4.31	PERS 3.86	ERD 4.10	PGR 4.18
PROD 4.55	MKTG 4.19	ERD 3.78	GADM 3.85	ERD 3.95
ERD 3.00	PGR 4.00	PROD 3.54	PROD 3.50	PROD 3.91
				$F = 3.22$

Total

N = 29	N = 104	N = 96	N = 20	N = 249

[a]Significant at $p < .01$ level.
[b]Significant at $p < .05$ level.

Note: LSD test between means statistically significant at $p < .05$ level.

Source: Compiled by the authors.

system, production had a significantly lower mean score than all other functions.

F-ratios for the repeated-measures AOVs for each of the three types of production system showed significance (at $p < .05$ level) in the case of the large-batch and mass- and continuous-process-production systems. On the other hand, the mean scores of the seven functions in the case of the unit-and-small-batch-production system were not significantly different.

The results of unweighted AOVs of the factorial design of grand corporate strategy $\times$ production system (see Table 6.4) for the mean strategic significance score of each function seem to indicate that the effect of grand corporate strategy was significant for all functions and that the effect of the production system was significant for general administration, engineering and R&D, and marketing. The interaction effect was not significant for any of the functions.

The F-ratios in one-way AOVs by production system (Table 6.2) did show significance for four functions: general administration, engineering and R&D, marketing, and public and government relations.

The results seem to indicate that the strategic significance of public and government relations varies when effects of strategy and production system are considered. For all other functions, when firms are classified by strategy and production system, the relative strategic significance of these functions seems to vary mainly because of the differences in their grand corporate strategy and not because of the differences in their production systems.

RESEARCH QUESTION 6

Research Question 6: For firms pursuing a particular grand corporate strategy, is the relative strategic significance of the seven organizational functions different for firms with varying types of organizational structures?

For this research question, the study's sample of 249 firms was categorized into 20 cells by means of a 5×4 factorial design of organizational structure $\times$ grand corporate strategy. As shown in Table 6.8, within each of the 20 cells, and the overall column and row cells, the seven organizational functions were ranked by their mean strategic significance scores. In the case of firms with stability and retrenchment strategies, the sample size in many cells was less than five.

The results of approximate LSD tests revealed significant differences in the mean scores of different functions for only a few cells. For firms with an external growth strategy, marketing had significantly higher mean scores than all the other functions in the geographic division and holding-company structures. In the case of a retrenchment strategy for firms whose organizational structure was functional with one or more divisions, marketing had a significantly higher mean score than all the other functions. For firms classified as functional with one or more product divisions or subsidiaries, general administration had a significantly higher, and production a significantly lower, mean score than all other functions. In the case of product division firms, general administration and finance had significantly higher mean scores than the other five functions, and production had a significantly lower mean score than all the other functions.

F-ratios for the repeated-measures AOVs for each of the five types of organizational structure showed significance in the case of only one type—product division. In other words, with the exception of product division, the mean scores of the seven functions in each type of organizational structure were not significantly different.

The results of one-way AOVs by organizational structures (Table 6.2) showed significance for only two functions: engineering and R&D and finance. The data, therefore, seem to indicate that for the other five functions there do not exist significant differences among their mean strategic significance scores attributable to organizational structure.

The results of unweighted AOVs for the entire factorial design of grand corporate strategy $\times$ organizational structure (Table 6.4) for the mean strategic significance score of each function seem to indicate that the effect of grand corporate strategy was significant for all functions except marketing, and the effect of organizational structure was not significant for any function. The interaction effect was significant for only three functions: personnel, public and government relations, and finance.

The results, therefore, seem to indicate that when industrial firms are classified by strategy and structure, the relative strategic significance of different functions seems to vary mainly because of the differences in their grand corporate strategies and not because of the differences in the type of organizational structure studied.

RESEARCH QUESTION 7

Research Question 7: For firms pursuing a particular grand corporate strategy, is the relative strategic significance of the seven organizational functions different for firms with varying perceived environmental uncertainty?

For this research question, the study's sample of 249 firms was categorized into cells by means of a factorial design of perceived environmental uncertainty (PEU) × grand corporate strategy. As shown in Table 6.9, within each cell the seven organizational functions were ranked by their mean strategic significance scores.

No a priori scheme exists for classifying executives' perceived environmental uncertainty into groups. Therefore, hierarchical cluster analysis was used to develop three groups of perceived environmental uncertainty (low, medium, and high). This technique allows the grouping of responses that are most similar to one another but most dissimilar to other groups. One respondent's score was so dissimilar from the others that it did not fit into any of the three groups. It, therefore, was deleted from the moderating analyses of perceived environmental uncertainty (it was also deleted from the analysis of production-system effects). The clustering procedure only permits the conclusion that the executives' PEU responses were high, medium, and low for this particular sample.

Differences between functional significance means scores were found in only four cells. Firms using an internal growth strategy with medium PEU had general administration ranked significantly higher, and marketing and production significantly lower, than other functions. General administration, marketing, and finance mean scores were significantly higher than other functions for firms using an external acquisitive growth strategy and with both medium and high PEU. In the external acquisitive growth-high PEU cell, production and engineering and R&D had significantly lower mean scores. In the retrenchment-medium PEU cell, marketing had a significantly higher mean score than other functions.

For all firms with a low PEU, general administration had a higher mean score than other functions. Engineering and R&D and production had lower mean scores for all firms with a high PEU. The most differences were found for all firms with a medium PEU. For these firms general administration was ranked highest, finance was second, and production ranked the lowest.

F-ratios for the repeated-measures AOVs for each of the three PEU groups indicated that the mean scores of the seven functions were significantly different in each of the PEU groups.

The results of one-way AOVs by PEU (Table 6.2) showed significance for only one function: marketing. Therefore, for the other six functions there do not seem to exist significant differences among their mean strategic significance scores attributable to the degree of PEU.

The results of unweighted AOVs for the entire factorial design of grand corporate strategy × PEU (Table 6.4) for the mean strategic significance score of each function seem to indicate that the effect of grand corporate strategy was significant for all functions. The effect of PEU was significant for marketing and personnel. The interaction

TABLE 6.9

Mean Functional Importance Scores of Organizational Functions: Grand Corporate Strategy by Perceived Environmental Uncertainty

Low PEU

	Stability	Internal Growth	External Acquisitive Growth	Retrenchment	All Firms
N =	6	19	7	1	32
	PGR 5.61	GADM 4.86	FIN 4.71	PGR 7.00	GADM 4.81
	GADM 5.00	PERS 4.61	MKTG 4.54	PERS 6.40	PGR 4.73
	FIN 4.77	FIN 4.59	GADM 4.52	PROD 5.00	FIN 4.58
	ERD 4.60	PGR 4.53	ERD 4.17	GADM 4.40	PERS 4.51
	PROD 4.58	ERD 4.28	PGR 4.11	MKTG 3.38	ERD 4.26
	PERS 4.47	PROD 4.05	PERS 3.93	FIN 2.50	PROD 4.10
	MKTG 4.40	MKTG 3.75	PROD 3.60	ERD 2.20	MKTG 4.01
					F = 2.84[a]

Medium PEU

	Stability	Internal Growth	External Acquisitive Growth	Retrenchment	All Firms
N =	19	66	53	15	153
	PGR 4.96	GADM 5.05	GADM 4.67	MKTG 4.49	GADM 4.78
	GADM 4.96	FIN 4.78	MKTG 4.66	FIN 4.03	FIN 4.62
	PERS 4.81	ERD 4.73	FIN 4.61	GADM 3.85	PERS 4.43
	FIN 4.57	PERS 4.68	PERS 4.19	PERS 3.69	MKTG 4.42
	ERD 4.55	PGR 4.62	PGR 4.09	ERD 3.37	PGR 4.35
	PROD 4.37	MKTG 4.25	ERD 4.03	PGR 3.29	ERD 4.33
	MKTG 4.28	PROD 4.15	PROD 3.84	PROD 3.28	PROD 3.98
					F = 11.32[b]

High PEU

	Stability	Internal Growth	External Acquisitive Growth	Retrenchment	All Firms
N =	4	19	36	4	63
	FIN 5.22	PERS 5.14	MKTG 4.86	MKTG 5.09	MKTG 4.85
	GADM 4.98	GADM 5.06	GADM 4.68	PERS 4.70	GADM 4.78
	PERS 4.70	PGR 5.03	FIN 4.62	FIN 4.56	FIN 4.71
	PROD 4.53	ERD 4.98	PGR 4.36	ERD 4.20	PERS 4.61
	MKTG 4.31	MKTG 4.90	PERS 4.30	GADM 4.15	PGR 4.52
	ERD 4.30	FIN 4.80	PROD 3.93	PROD 3.95	ERD 4.19
	PGR 3.83	PROD 4.45	ERD 3.77		PROD 4.12
					F = 7.23[b]

Total

	Stability	Internal Growth	External Acquisitive Growth	Retrenchment	All Firms
N =	29	104	95	20	248

[a] p < .05.
[b] p < .01.

Note: LSD test between means statistically significant at p < .05.

Source: Compiled by the authors.

effect was significant for public and government relations and personnel.

The results, therefore, seem to indicate that when firms are
classified by strategy and PEU, the relative strategic significance of
different functions seems to vary mainly because of the differences
in their grand corporate strategy and not because of the differences
in the degree of PEU.

ANALYSES OF DATA NOT DIRECTLY RELATED
TO THE RESEARCH OBJECTIVES

For this study, as explained in Chapter 3, the responding senior
executives were not asked to evaluate each of the seven functions in
terms of its strategic significance on a Likert-type rating scale. In-
stead, a normative list of 55 key result areas (grouped under seven
organizational functions) was developed and the senior executives
were asked to rate each key result area separately in terms of its
strategic significance to effective implementation of the firm's grand
corporate strategy. The evaluation of each key result area was based
upon a seven-point rating scale from 1 to 7. For each firm the strategic significance of each function was based on the average of the
ratings of key result areas in that functional category.

Although the focus of this study is on the strategic significance
mix of different functions rather than the strategic significance mix
of different key result areas, it was thought that additional analyses
by key result areas would provide some interesting and useful data.
The top 16 key result areas, ranked by their mean strategic significance scores, are listed in Table 6.10. Each of the seven functions
is represented in this list of top 16 (out of a total of 55) key result
areas.

As shown in Table 6.1 general administration had the highest
strategic significance among all functions for the overall sample.
The analysis by key result areas makes this fact even more obvious.
Three out of the top four and five out of the top ten key result areas
are from the general administration category. Interestingly enough,
out of the five general administration key result areas (shown in Table
6.10), the following three directly relate to the area of business
policy and strategic planning.

1. Ability to perceive new business opportunities and potential
threats,

2. Achieving a better overall control of general corporate
performance,

3. Developing a more effective companywide strategic planning
system for planned overall corporate development.

TABLE 6.10

The Top 16 Key Result Areas Ranked by Their Mean Strategic Significance Scores

(N = 249)

Key Result Area			Mean Strategic Significance Score
1.	GADM	1	Attracting and retaining well-trained and competent top managers	6.06
2.	MKTG	33	Maintaining a highly trained, motivated, vigorous, and dynamic sales organization	5.82
3.	GADM	3	Ability to perceive new business opportunities and potential threats	5.47
4.	GADM	2	Achieving a better overall control of general corporate performance	5.33
5.	FIN	38	Sound capital structure allowing flexibility to raise additional capital for internal growth and acquisitions	5.26
6.	GADM	5	Ability to unify conflicting opinions, improve coordination and enhance effective collaboration between key executives, generate enthusiasm, and motivate sufficient managerial drive for growth and profits	5.15
7.	ERD	21	Improvement in research and new product development capabilities	5.08
8.	MKTG	27	Widening the customer base by intensive market penetration and development	5.06
9.	FIN	34	Improving bond ratings and common stock market performance	5.00
10.	GADM	6	Developing a more effective companywide strategic planning system for planned overall corporate development	5.00
11.	PROD	11	An ongoing plant modernization program to keep the efficiency of equipment comparable to that of the major competitors	4.87
12.	FIN	39	Strong working capital position allowing flexibility to raise short-term capital at low cost	4.84
13.	PERS	48	Improved employee motivation, job satisfaction, and morale	4.84
14.	PERS	49	Stimulating and rewarding creativity in employees and installing incentive performance reward systems	4.79
15.	PERS	46	Effective and efficient personnel policies for hiring, training, promotion, compensation, and employee services	4.79
16.	PGR	55	Improving overall corporate image	4.77

Source: Compiled by the authors.

CONCLUSION

    This chapter has presented the results of analyses of data collected for the study. The strategic mixes of organizational functions for effective implementation of different grand corporate strategies have been identified. Statistical tests clearly indicate that there do exist significant differences among the mean strategic significance scores of the functions attributable to grand corporate strategies pursued by the firms. The collective perceptions of the senior executives in industrial firms seem to suggest that the relative strategic significance of the seven different organizational functions is different for firms pursuing varying grand corporate strategies.

    When the influence of firm size, corporate diversity, industry, production system, organizational structure, and perceived environmental uncertainty were considered for each type of grand corporate strategy, the strategic mixes of organizational functions were found to be different. The analyses by grand corporate strategy and each of the mediating variables indicated that the grand corporate strategy was responsible for most of the explained variance of mean strategic significance scores of different organizational functions.

    With the results of the study having been presented, the next chapter will fully discuss these results, provide a summary of findings, and present some conclusions.

7

DISCUSSION
OF RESULTS,
SUMMARY, AND
CONCLUSIONS

This chapter presents a discussion of the results of the study's empirical analyses of data. It provides a summary of the findings; and a conclusion to this chapter summarizes the salient features of the importance of this study and the implications for further research.

DISCUSSION OF RESULTS

At the outset, it is important to reiterate that this study's conceptual framework is not a theory in the strict sense of the term. This study is exploratory in nature, and the aim is to develop a better understanding of the concept of corporate strategy. It has integrated several different concepts from the fields of corporate strategy and organization theory. The primary thrust of this study is to investigate the relationships between grand corporate strategies pursued and the strategic mixes of seven organizational functions in industrial firms. The secondary thrust of this study is to identify the nature of the influence of size, corporate diversity, industry type, production system, organizational structure, and perceived environmental uncertainty on the interrelationships between the grand corporate strategy pursued and the relative importance of different functional tasks. Thus, the aim of the study is to provide the understanding to determine the relationships that exist; therefore, no cause-and-effect conclusions can be drawn. The discussion in this section will be broken down according to the major areas of the study.

RELATIVE STRATEGIC SIGNIFICANCE OF
DIFFERENT ORGANIZATIONAL FUNCTIONS

For the entire sample of 249 industrial firms, the mean strategic significance score of the top-ranked general administration was significantly higher than the remaining six functions (Table 6.1). Finance was ranked second. Personnel, marketing, and public and government relations (ranked third) had mean strategic significance scores not significantly different from one another. The fourth place went to engineering and R&D. Production was ranked last among the seven functions, with its mean strategic significance score significantly lower than all the others.

As shown in Table 6.10, the key result areas included under the general administration category account for five of the top ten. Of these five key result areas, the first relates to the ability to attract and retain competent top managers; the second relates to the leadership role of general management in a large organization; and the remaining three directly relate to the area of business policy and planning. These findings empirically affirm the paramount importance of the general administration function in large industrial firms. It also highlights top management interest and involvement in strategic planning. It seems that the prognosis by many management writers that the decade of the 1970s would go down in the management history as the "decade of strategic planning" may be true. It also suggests that the current upsurge in the academic interest in "strategic management" is also very timely, and none too soon. A need for a clear dichotomy between strategic and operating management has never been greater.

The highest importance given to general adminstration seems to support the findings of Stevenson (1968) and Steiner (1969a). The identification of finance as the second most important function highlights the important contribution that the chief financial officer can make to a large industrial firm. It supports Pohl's (1973) contention that the trend toward an increase in the direct involvement of the chief financial officers in the strategic issues handled by top management is likely to continue.

Godiwalla, Meinhart, and Warde (1979), in their study of the influence of functional managements (general management excluded) on the overall corporate strategy, found marketing, finance, and production to be the three most crucial functions in order of importance. In this study, after general administration, finance had the highest strategic significance, followed by personnel, marketing, and public and government relations. Production, on the other hand, had the lowest strategic significance. The study's analyses, therefore, do

TABLE 7.1

Rankings of the Seven Organizational Functions Based on the Managerial Perceptions of
Their Strategic Significance

	Sample Number	Organizational Functions						
		GADM	PROD	ERD	MKTG	FIN	PERS	PGR
1. In firms pursuing different grand corporate strategies								
Stability	29	1	6	5	7	4	3	2
Internal growth	104	1	7	4	6	2	3	5
External acquisitive growth	96	2	7	6	1	3	4	5
Retrenchment	20	4	6	7	1	2	3	5
2. In firms with different size (annual sales revenue in millions of dollars)								
200 and less	60	1	5	6	2	4	3	7
201-599	84	1	7	6	4	3	2	5
600 and over	105	1	7	4	6	2	5	3
3. In firms with different degrees of corporate diversity								
Single business firms	28	1	6	7	5	3	2	4
Dominant business firms	55	1	7	5	2	4	3	6
Related business firms	116	1	7	6	4	2	3	5
Unrelated business firms	50	1	6	5	3	2	4	7
4. In firms in different industries								
Consumer nondurable goods	73	1	7	6	4	2	5	3
Consumer durable goods	34	2	7	3	1	4	5	6
Capital goods	61	1	6	5	2	3	4	7
Producer goods	81	1	7	5	6	2	3	4
5. In firms with different types of production systems								
Unit and small batch	41	1	6	5	3	2	4	7
Large batch and mass	137	1	7	6	3	2	4	5
Continuous process	70	1	7	6	5	2	4	3
6. In firms with different types of organizational structure								
Functional	28	1	5	7	3	4	2	6
Functional with one or more product divisions or subsidiaries	57	1	7	6	4	3	2	5
Product division	111	1	7	5	3	2	4	6
Geographic division	32	1	7	6	3	4	2	5
Holding company	21	1	7	6	2	3	4	5
7. In firms facing different degrees of perceived environmental uncertainty								
Low	33	1	6	5	7	3	4	2
Medium	153	1	7	6	4	2	3	5
High	63	2	7	6	1	3	4	5
All firms (overall)	249	1	7	6	4	2	3	5

Source: Compiled by the authors.

not support their findings. The lowest rank of production seems to
support Heau's (1976) contention that it is only in the case of vertically
integrated firms that the top management is production oriented.

To sum up, the aggregate analyses of data clearly indicate that
the relative strategic significance of the seven functions is different
in industrial firms. The data were further analyzed by grand corporate strategy, size, corporate diversity, industry, production system, organizational structure, and perceived environmental uncertainty. Table 7.1 shows the rankings of functions in different schemes
of classification. It might be pointed out that general administration
had the top rank in all but a few subgroups. In the next seven sections
the results of the analyses of data by strategy, size, diversity, industry, production system, organizational structure, and PEU are discussed separately.

Analysis by Grand Corporate Strategy

When the aggregate data were analyzed by grand corporate strategy, the strategic mixes of organizational functions were found to be
different for each strategy type. As shown in Table 6.1, only in the
case of retrenchment strategy (marketing) did the top-ranked function
have a significantly higher score than all the other functions. In the
case of external growth strategy, marketing, general administration,
and finance had significantly higher scores than the remaining five
functions. For internal growth strategy firms there were no differences between the five top-ranked functions (general administration,
finance, personnel, engineering and R&D, and public and government
relations). We can therefore conclude that general administration
and finance appear to be critical functions for both internal and external growth strategies, whereas marketing is a critical function for retrenchment and external growth strategies. There seems to be no one
or two critical functions for firms pursuing a stability strategy; although in line with the aggregate data, general administration seems
to be strategically very important. The data also seem to indicate
relatively higher importance for public and government relations in
the case of firms pursuing a stability strategy.

Statistical analyses discussed in the previous chapter clearly
indicate that the effect of grand corporate strategy on the relative
strategic importance of the seven functions is highly significant; it
is more significant than the effect of any other mediating variable to
be discussed later in this chapter. Almost every function is significantly affected by the grand corporate strategy pursued. It is, therefore, extremely important for large firms changing grand corporate
strategy to reevaluate the priority of critical functions; otherwise
the effective implementation of the new grand corporate strategy is

likely to be hampered. These findings seem to support Allen's (1972) study of the differences in conglomerates and vertically integrated companies, Heau's (1976) study of the critical functions in vertically integrated and conglomerate firms, and Miles and Snow's (1978) typology of organizations with distinguishing features consistent with the organizational strategies.

Effect of Size

Table 6.3 shows the effect on the strategic mixes of organizational functions when firms in each of the four strategy groups are further analyzed by their size. For each strategy group, the rankings of functions in different size categories are different.

In the case of a stability strategy, the effect of size seems to be the most pronounced for public and government relations, and finance seems to have a relatively higher importance in small firms. However, the least significant difference (LSD) tests revealed no significant differences in the mean scores of the different functions in any size category.

For firms pursuing an internal growth strategy, general administration seems to be very important irrespective of firm size. However, the LSD tests showed significant differences in mean scores only in the case of large firms; the lowest-ranked production and marketing had mean scores significantly lower than the remaining five functions.

For firms pursuing an external growth strategy, the results of LSD tests indicate that (1) production had a mean score significantly lower than all the other six functions in the case of large firms and (2) general administration and marketing had mean scores significantly higher than the remaining five functions in the case of medium-sized firms. In the case of small firms LSD tests showed no significant differences. The data seem to suggest that marketing and general administration are very important functions irrespective of firm size. There seem to be no one or two critical functions for firms pursuing retrenchment strategies, although, in line with the aggregate data, marketing seems to be strategically very important.

The results unweighted factorial analysis of variances (AOVs) show that when firms pursuing different grand corporate strategies were subclassified by size, the effect of size on the relative importance of functional tasks was most pronounced on two functions: engineering and R&D and public and government relations. For the other five functions the effect of size showed no significance (at $p < .05$ level). On the other hand, the effect of grand corporate strategy was significant for all functions. Therefore, grand corporate strategy seems responsible for most of the explained variance of mean strategic significance scores for different organizational functions.

The findings of this study with regard to the effect of size should be interpreted with caution. The study's sample came from a population of the 1,000 largest U.S. industrial firms, the smallest of which had annual sales exceeding $100 million. Therefore, the terms small and medium (used in this study to distinguish firms in the sample by size) have rather specific meanings. This might also be an important reason why the results do not seem to support the importance of size as a contextual variable, as suggested by many organization theorists.

Effect of Corporate Diversity

Table 6.5 shows the effect on the strategic mixes of organizational functions when firms in each of the four strategy groups are further analyzed by corporate diversity. For each strategy group, the rankings of functions in different diversity categories are different.

In the case of a stability strategy, public and government relations and engineering and R&D seem to be most affected by differences in the degree of corporate diversity. However, the LSD tests did not reveal any significant differences in the mean scores for any of the four cells.

In the case of an internal growth strategy, general administration was the critical function for the related business firms. The importance of engineering and R&D seemed to increase with diversity.

In the case of an external growth strategy, the analysis by diversity did not seem to change the importance of marketing, general administration, and finance. Marketing and general administration were the most strategic functions in the dominant business firms. Marketing, general administration, and finance were the most strategic functions in related and unrelated business firms.

In the case of a retrenchment strategy, marketing was given the highest importance in the related business firms. In the other three cells, the LSD tests did not reveal any significant differences, although the overall trends seem to suggest that marketing is a crucial function irrespective of the degree of corporate diversity.

The results of unweighted factorial AOV's show that when firms pursuing different grand corporate strategies were subclassified by the degree of corporate diversity, the effect of corporate diversity was most pronounced on public and government relations, and the interaction effect (of corporate diversity and grand corporate strategy) was most pronounced on public and government relations and engineering and R&D. On the other hand, the effect of grand corporate strategy was significant for all functions except marketing.

The relative strategic significance of marketing, therefore, does not seem to change in industrial firms when their grand corporate strategies and their degree of diversity are taken into account. On the other hand, differences in strategy and diversity seem to have a considerable influence on the relative strategic significance of public and government relations and engineering and R&D in industrial firms. For general administration, production-operations, finance, and personnel, strategy and not diversity seems responsible for most of the differences in their relative strategic significance.

The studies by Chandler (1962), Fouraker and Stopford (1968), Galbraith and Nathanson (1978), Khandwalla (1974), Miller and Springate (1978), and Rumelt (1974) found systematic structural differences in firms pursuing different diversification strategies; however, the data for this study do not show any systematic differences in the relative strategic importance of different functional tasks when firms in different strategy groups are further analyzed by corporate diversity.

Effect of Industry

Table 6.6 shows the effect on the strategic mixes of organizational functions when firms in each of the four strategy groups are further analyzed by industry. In the case of a stability strategy, engineering and R&D, public and government relations, and personnel seemed to be most affected by differences in industry types.

In the case of an internal growth strategy, engineering and R&D seemed to have a relatively higher importance in the consumer durable goods industries.

In the case of an external growth strategy, the analysis by industry showed little difference. The results of LSD tests showed that marketing, general administration, and finance were critical functions in the capital- and producer-goods industries.

In the case of a retrenchment strategy, the LSD tests did not reveal any significance in any of the four cells. This, coupled with the small sample size in each cell, precludes any generalization.

The results of unweighted factorial AOVs show that when firms pursuing different grand corporate strategies were subclassified by industry, the effect of industry was significant only in production and marketing, and the interaction effect was significant only in the case of general administration. The effect of grand corporate strategy was, however, significant for all functions except marketing.

To conclude, the differences in strategy and industry have a significant effect on the relative importance of production. The relative strategic significance of marketing seems to be affected by the differences in industry rather than by differences in strategy. For the remaining five functions, contrary to the findings of Lawrence and Lorsch (1967a) and Miles and Snow (1978), strategy, not industry, seems to be responsible for most of the differences in their relative importance.

Effect of Production System

Table 6.7 shows the effect on the strategic mixes of organizational functions when firms in each strategy group are further analyzed by production system. No differences in functional mean scores were found in stability/production system cells.

In the case of an internal growth strategy, the analyses by LSD tests indicated general administration to be the most strategic function and production the least strategic function in the mass production system; marketing was the least strategic function in the continuous-process production system.

In the case of an external growth strategy, further analysis by production system did not show any major changes, the results of LSD tests showed that marketing, general administration, and finance were the critical functions in the mass production and in the continuous-process production systems, with engineering and R&D and production the least critical functions with continuous-process systems.

In the case of a retrenchment strategy, LSD tests did not reveal any critical function(s); however, marketing seemed to be very important, irrespective of the type of production system.

The results of unweighted factorial AOVs show that when firms pursuing different grand corporate strategies were subclassified by production system, the effect of production system was significant only in public and government relations; the effect of grand corporate strategy was significant for all seven functions but marketing; and the interaction effect was not significant in any function.

Therefore, differences in strategy and production system have a significant effect on the relative importance of public and government relations; on the other hand, differences in strategy and production system do not seem to influence the relative importance of marketing in industrial firms. For the other five functions, strategy and not production system seems responsible for most of the differences in their relative importance.

As per the findings of such organizational theorists as Woodward (1965), Thompson (1967), Hickson, Pugh, and Pheysey (1969), Perrow (1970), and Murphy (1972), the firm's predominant production system affects the structural and scale (size) aspects of the organization. The analyses of the study's data seem to indicate that compared with the grand corporate strategy, the production system seems to have considerably less influence on the relative importance of different functional tasks.

Effect of Organizational Structure

Table 6.8 shows the effect on the strategic mixes of organizational functions when firms in each of four strategy groups are further analyzed by organizational structure. In the case of firms with stability and retrenchment strategies, the strategic mixes of functions were different in different types of structures; however, the extremely small sample sizes make the generalizations of findings rather questionable.

For firms pursuing a retrenchment strategy, the results of LSD tests showed marketing to be the most strategic function in firms with structures that were functional with one or more product divisions or subsidiaries.

In the case of an internal growth strategy, the relative strategic significance of different functions seemed to change with structure, but general administration seemed to have very high strategic significance irrespective of the type of organizational structure.

In the case of an external growth strategy, marketing was the most strategic function for firms with both the geographic division and the holding-company structures.

The results of unweighted factorial AOVs show that when firms pursuing different grand corporate strategies were subclassified by organizational structure, the effect of organizational structure was not significant for any function; the effect of grand corporate strategy was significant for all functions except marketing; and the interaction effect was significant for finance, personnel, and public and government relations.

Therefore, differences in strategy and organizational structure do not seem to have any effect on the relative strategic significance of marketing in industrial firms. For the other six functions, strategy and not organizational structure seems responsible for most of the differences in their relative importance.

The major research findings in the area of organizational theory highlight the importance of organizational structure as a crucial contextual variable; the business-policy research findings also consider structure as a crucial variable in the area of strategy implementation. However, the analyses of the study's data seem to indicate that organizational structure does not have any significant influence on the relative importance of different functions in large industrial firms.

Effect of Perceived Environmental Uncertainty (PEU)

Table 6.9 shows the effect on the strategic mixes of organizational functions when firms in each of the four strategy groups are
further analyzed by perceived environmental uncertainty (PEU).

Care must be taken in generalizing the results for firms pursuing
stability and retrenchment strategies, for firms with high and low PEU
because of very small sample sizes. No functional mean scores were
significantly different in these cells.

For the two growth strategies, analyses by PEU showed no differences in the strategic mixes of functions for low PEU and only a
few for high PEU. The results of LSD tests showed that in the case of
firms pursuing external growth strategies, marketing, general administration, and finance were the critical functions for firms with a
high PEU.

The most functional mean score differences were found for firms
with a medium PEU. In the internal growth cell, general administration was the most critical and marketing and production the least critical functions. In the external growth cell, general administration,
marketing, and finance were the critical functions. Marketing was
the critical function for retrenchment strategy firms with a medium
PEU. These results conflict with previous research (for example,
Miles and Snow [1978]), which suggests that most differences would
occur for high-PEU firms. These results may have occurred because
few have examined the variables in the manner of the study described
herein. Previous studies have largely ignored firms with a medium
PEU; rather, they separate firms into only high and low groups (for
example, Miles and Snow [1978]).

The results of unweighted factorial AOVs show that when firms
pursuing different grand corporate strategies were subclassified by
PEU, the effect of PEU was significant for only two functions, marketing and personnel; the effect of grand corporate strategy was significant for all functions; and the interaction effect was significant
for public and government relations and personnel. Therefore, differences in strategy seem responsible for most of the differences in
the relative importance of the functions, but PEU has some effect.
The results do not support the findings of Lawrence and Lorsch (1967b)
and Miles and Snow (1978) regarding the effect of PEU on the relative
strategic importance of different functions.

Analysis of Firm Size

The analysis of aggregate data by size (Table 6.3, overall row
cells) revealed differences in the strategic mixes of functions for
different sizes. General administration had the highest mean stra-

tegic significance scores in all size categories, although LSD tests revealed significance only for the small and medium-size categories. The results of LSD tests also showed that marketing had the lowest strategic importance in large firms. The relative importance of finance and public and government relations seemed to increase with size, whereas the importance of marketing declined with the increase in size. Large firms also gave more importance to engineering and R&D and less importance to personnel.

The results of one-way AOVs by size indicated significance for engineering and R&D, finance, and public and government relations. Therefore, the relative strategic significance of each of these three functions seems to vary with size. Conversely, the relative strategic significance of general administration, production, marketing, and personnel does not seem to change with the change in size.

Godiwalla's (1977) findings regarding the strategic functional managements in firms of different sizes are not comparable with this study's findings because of the differences in the definition of size.

Analysis by Corporate Diversity

The analysis of aggregate data by corporate diversity (Table 6.5, overall row cells) did show changes in the strategic mixes of organizational functions for different degrees of corporate diversity. The results of LSD tests showed that for related business firms general administration had the highest strategic significance, and production had the lowest strategic significance. No significant differences in the mean scores were observed for the other three diversity categories.

However, the results of one-way AOVs by corporate diversity showed significance in the case of only two functions: engineering and R&D and public and government relations. Thus, significant differences do exist in the relative importance of these two functions attributable to corporate diversity. Conversely, in industrial firms the relative importance of general administration, production, marketing, finance, and personnel does not seem to vary with a change in the degree of corporate diversity.

Analysis by Industry

The analysis of aggregate data by industry (Table 6.6, overall row cells) revealed differences in the strategic mixes of organizational functions for different industries. The results of LSD tests showed that general administration had the highest strategic significance in the capital and producer goods industries, and production had the lowest strategic significance in the consumer nondurable and producer goods industries. Public and government relations had higher importance in the consumer nondurable goods industry. Marketing seemed more important in the consumer durable and capital goods industries.

The results of one-way AOVs by industry showed significance for production and marketing; therefore, we would expect the relative strategic importance of production and marketing to differ in different industries. Thus, the relative strategic importance of general administration, engineering and R&D, finance, personnel, and public and government relations in industrial firms seems to remain the same irrespective of the type of industry.

The study's findings do not seem to support the conclusions from Miles and Snow's (1978) study. According to them, the chief executives' ranking of the top three functions were different in food processing and electronics industries. In the food processing industry, the top three functions were sales and marketing, production, and long-range planning. According to data from this study, in the consumer nondurable goods industries general administration (including long-range planning) was found to have the highest mean score; marketing had the fourth highest mean score; and production was the least important function.

According to Lawrence and Lorsch (1967b), ". . . marketing had more influence than production in both container-manufacturing and food-processing firms, apparently because of its involvement in (uncertain) innovations and with customers" (Hickson, Hinnings, Lee, Schneck, and Pennings 1971, p. 219). This study's findings indicate that marketing had higher mean scores than production in all four types of industries.

Analysis by Production System

The analysis of aggregate data by production system (Table 6.7, overall row cells) showed changes in the strategic mixes of functions for different production systems. General administration had the highest rank in the unit and small-batch and mass-production systems; for the continuous-process production system, the LSD tests showed no significant differences in the mean scores of different functions. Apparently, senior executives do not consider the production function to be strategically important to effective implementation of grand corporate strategies. In the case of mass- and process-production systems, production had the lowest strategic importance.

The results of one-way AOVs by production system showed significance for general administration, engineering and R&D, marketing, and public and government relations. Therefore, it seems significant differences do exist in the relative importance of these functions attributable to production system. Conversely, the relative importance of production, finance, and personnel does not seem to vary with change in the production system. The most surprising result is that the differences in the predominant production system do not seem to have any effect on the perceptions of senior executives in industrial firms about the relative strategic significance of the production function.

Woodward (1965) identified development, production, and marketing as the critical functions for unit and small-batch, large-batch, mass-, and continuous-process production systems, respectively. The study's findings do not support Woodward's conclusions; none of the three functions were found to be "critical" for any type of production system. In fact, for a mass-production system, the production function not only had the lowest rank but also had a mean score significantly lower than all the other functions. If Woodward's three functions alone were considered for each of the three types of production systems, the rank ordering was marketing, development, and production.

The study's findings also partially support Godiwalla's (1977) findings about the influence of functional managements on overall corporate strategy in firms with different production systems. Godiwalla found marketing and finance to be the two top functions for all three types of production systems. However, the data from this study indicate similar results only for the unit and small-batch type. Finance and marketing were relatively important functions in mass production (in the second group). The relative importance of R&D and production identified by Godiwalla also differs from this study's findings.

Analysis by Organizational Structure

The analysis of aggregate data by organizational structure (Table 6.8, overall row cells) revealed no major changes. The top four functions in all types of organizational structures (not necessarily in that order) were general administration, finance, personnel, and marketing.

The results of one-way AOVs by organizational structure showed significance for only two functions: finance and engineering and R&D. Therefore, barring these two functions, the relative importance of functional tasks in industrial firms does not seem to vary with their organizational structures.

Analysis by Perceived Environmental Uncertainty

The analysis of aggregate data by perceived environmental uncertainty (Table 6.9, overall row cells) revealed a few changes. General administration was the critical function for firms with a low PEU. For firms with a high PEU, marketing was ranked in the highest group. Therefore, a high degree of PEU seems to increase the relative strategic significance of marketing in industrial firms. The results of one-way AOVs by PEU showed significance in only one function: marketing. Thus, with the exception of marketing, differences in the degree of perceived environmental uncertainty do not seem to influence the perceptions of senior executives in industrial firms regarding the strategic significance of different functional tasks.

Most effects of PEU were found for firms with a medium PEU. It should also be noted that a majority of the firms in the sample (153 out of 249) had a medium PEU. General administration was most critical; finance, second; and production, last for these firms.

The study's findings do not quite support Miles and Snow's (1978) contention that firms facing a high PEU place greater emphasis on externally oriented functions like product development and market research. Although, the firms facing a high PEU considered marketing important; the same phenomenon was not observed for engineering and R&D and public and government relations.

SUMMARY OF FINDINGS

The central point of the study's findings indicates that general administration is perceived by the senior executives as having the highest strategic significance in industrial firms. The strategic significance score of general administration was the highest among all functions. Approximate LSD tests showed that the mean score for general administration was significantly higher than for all other functions. Finance was the second highest. The next three strategically important functions were personnel, marketing, and public and government relations. As a group, their mean scores were significantly higher than those of the last three functions. Next was engineering and R&D; and production was found to be strategically the least important function in industrial firms.

Analysis by grand corporate strategy showed that strategic mixes of functions were different for the four types of grand corporate strategies. For stability strategy, no differences in functional mean scores were found. For internal growth strategy, LSD tests showed that marketing and production had significantly lower mean scores than all other functions, with no other differences occurring. For external acquisitve growth strategy, the top three functions were marketing, general administration, and finance. For retrenchment strategy, marketing had a mean score significantly higher than those of all other functions. One-way AOVs by grand corporate strategy showed significance in the case of all functions. The relative strategic significance of each of the seven functions is therefore different for firms pursuing different grand corporate strategies. It must be mentioned that the study finds grand corporate strategies to be more important than all other organizational variables.

The influence of size as a mediating variable was assessed through unweighted factorial AOVs of size × strategy. The effect of strategy was found to be significant for all functions. The effect of size, however, was limited to only two functions: engineering and R&D and public and government relations. The interaction effect was significant for all functions except finance.

The results of unweighted AOVs of corporate diversity × strategy showed that the effect of strategy was significant for all functions except marketing; the effect of corporate diversity was significant only for public and government relations. The interaction effect showed significance only for engineering and R&D and public and government relations.

The results of unweighted factorial AOVs of industry × strategy showed that the effect of strategy was significant for all functions except marketing. The effect of industry was significant for only production and marketing, and the interaction effect was significant only for general administration.

The results of unweighted factorial AOVs of production system × strategy again showed the effect of strategy to be significant for all functions. The effect of the production system showed significance for general administration, engineering and R&D, and marketing; and the interaction effect showed no significance for any function.

The results of unweighted factorial AOVs of organizational structure × strategy showed that the effect of strategy was significant for all functions except marketing. The effect of organizational structure was not significant for any function; however, the interaction effect was significant for finance, personnel, and public and government relations.

Finally, the results of unweighted factorial AOVs of perceived environmental uncertainty × strategy showed that the effect of strategy was significant for all functions. The interaction effect was significant only for public and government relations and personnel, and the effect of PEU was significant for marketing and personnel.

The statistical analyses, therefore, clearly indicate that the relative strategic importance of different functions is affected more by grand corporate strategy than by any other organizational characteristic. The grand corporate strategy affected the strategic significance of all seven functions; the other organizational variables affected the strategic significance of some of the functions.

To summarize, the relative strategic importance of general administration varies significantly in industrial firms pursuing different strategies and having different production systems. The relative strategic importance of production varies significantly in firms with different strategies and in different industries. The relative strategic importance of engineering and R&D varies significantly with differences in strategy, size, corporate diversity, production system, and organizational structure. The relative strategic importance of marketing varies significantly with differences in strategy, industry, production system, and PEU. The relative strategic importance of finance varies significantly with differences in strategy, size, and organizational structure. The relative strategic importance of personnel seems to be affected by strategy and PEU. And finally, the relative strategic importance of public and government relations varies significantly in industrial firms with differences in strategy, size, corporate diversity, production system, and PEU.

CONCLUSIONS

This business-policy research has sought to identify the strategic mixes of organizational functions in industrial firms pursuing different grand corporate strategies. It has also sought to identify differences in the strategic mixes of organizational functions between firms pursuing a particular grand corporate strategy classified by their size, corporate diversity, industry, production system, organizational structure, and perceived environmental uncertainty. The data for this study were obtained from senior executives of large U.S. industrial corporations. Their collective experiences, judgments, and insights have endowed the research findings with the verisimilitude of the real world of business.

The contingency approach of this study recognizes that the relative strategic significance of different functional tasks cannot be the same in all types of industrial firms. However, there are definable patterns of relationships for different types of industrial firms that can be empirically determined. The central concept derived from the study's findings suggests that there is no one universally effective strategic mix of organizational functions for all industrial firms. The nature and content of the strategic mix of functions for a firm would depend upon the nature of some key organizational characteristics, the most important of which, as the study's findings indicate, is the firm's grand corporate strategy. The strategic mix of functions is one that is perceived to be essential for the effective implementation of the grand corporate strategy pursued by a firm during a particular time frame.

This section will provide a discussion of the implications of the study's findings, suggestions for future research, and concluding statements.

Implications of the Findings

Implications for Theory

This research has identified the nature of the contribution of each functional task to effective implementation of different grand corporate strategies in industrial firms facing different contingencies. It has enriched the field of corporate strategy by integrating certain key concepts from organization theory and behavior. It has also provided empirical support for the integrative approach to the study of corporate strategy through the identification of strategic mixes of organizational functions. Business-policy courses are designed to provide the students with, among other things, a means for functional integration. This study has attempted to integrate the different fields of management by identifying critical functional tasks; however, its research approach is based more on functional decomposition rather than functional integration. Its aim was to determine the relative strategic significance of different functions for effective implementation of grand corporate strategies in industrial firms facing different contingencies.

The functional approach to the study of corporate strategy is of a very recent origin. The results of the study provide important contributions to the existing body of knowledge regarding the influence of grand corporate strategy, size, corporate diversity, industry, production system, organizational structure, and perceived environmental uncertainty on the strategic mixes of functions in industrial firms. The influence of grand corporate strategy appears to be the most crucial among these different contingencies. The study has also provided empirical evidence that, contrary to certain expectations, the degree of perceived environmental uncertainty does not by itself influence the firm's strategic mix of functions.

The study has been largely of an exploratory nature but contains several questions that have differing degrees of theoretical and empirical support. It has provided a research methodology for integrating, interdisciplinary, and exploratory research using the functional approach to the study of grand corporate strategy and has thereby opened many research avenues to the study of grand strategy in other business and nonbusiness organizations.

Implications for Organizational Practices

Aside from the preceding implications for theory and research, there are some significant implications for organizational practice that may be based on the results of the study. The study's findings are based on the perceptions of the senior executives of large industrial firms and thus are likely to be of interest to all practicing managers. Depending upon the nature of contingencies facing the firm, its senior executives can compare their strategic mix of functions with those identified by the senior executives participating in this study. This will help practicing managers become aware of the key strategic functions in their firms and induce them to search for possible reasons for a particular strategic mix; this might require identification of strategic key result areas in each functional task, as well as the establishment of an ongoing information system for close monitoring.

The identification of strategic key result areas for a particular firm would be similar to the management audit. Since most senior executives are pressed for time, their concentration on the strategically significant areas would not only result in the more productive use of top management time, but would also result in the more effective implementation of chosen strategy and better overall corporate performance. Steiner (1969a) points out the following:

> By identifying the majority of strategic factors which businessmen themselves think are most important in their firm's success, the basis will be laid for a more systematic evaluation of these factors by each executive to find that combination which, when identified and followed, will enhance the fortunes of his company and benefit all those interested in its well-being. [P. 56]

The contingency approach of this study has another significant implication for practicing executives. If a change occurs in any of the major organizational characteristics (grand corporate strategy, diversity, industry, and so on), it certainly calls for a reassessment of the firm's strategic mix of functions (and also strategic key result areas in different functions), although it may or may not necessitate a realignment of functional priorities. This is necessary even when (or if you prefer, especially when) the firm has a formal planning system. As Allison (1971) points out, "Long range planning tends to become institutionalized and then disregarded" (Heau 1976, p. 12).

The foregoing remarks indicate the importance of identifying strategic mixes of functions for effective implementation of grand strategy at the corporate level. However, similar processes of identification of strategic functions and key result areas could be extremely beneficial at the division level, as well as at the business level within a division. For large divisionalized firms this may in fact be essential.

The specific findings of this study also have some significant implications for management practitioners. The identification of marketing as the most critical function for firms pursuing retrenchment strategies has a very clear message to the top executives. For such firms a reduction in resources allocated to the marketing function as a part of an across-the-board cost reduction program may prove to be counterproductive. Especially in the early stages of the problems, such firms may in fact want to strengthen their marketing function. This action might be an effective turnaround strategy in the long run.

The identification of general administration as the most critical function in most types of industrial firms highlights the importance of strategic planning and management, in general, and planning for top management manpower, in particular. Most managers require some broadening in order to be effective generalists; and the chief executive officers, personnel managers, and management training and development managers need to be cognizant of this phenomenon. In fact, awareness and understanding of top management's functions and responsibilities should be the single most important criterion for determining the promotability of a functional manager. The findings of the study seem to emphasize this point especially for production executives; most senior executives do not regard production as a critical function. The production executives can, therefore, increase their visibility for promotion to top management positions by increasing their knowledge and experience in the area of general management. This holds true for all young managers in quest of self-development who aspire to be chief executive officers.

Implications for Business Educators

The implications of the findings for business educators are even more obvious. The development of student awareness and understanding of general management functions and responsibilities is one sure way of developing tomorrow's business leaders. According to Tavernier (1979), the Royal Dutch/Shell Group is convinced it can identify managers with the potential for senior-level promotion on the strength of only four basic qualities.

> These are: the power of analysis, imagination, a sense
> of reality and the "helicopter" quality, the ability to look
> at facts and problems from an overall viewpoint. . . .
> The helicopter quality, which has become the hallmark
> of successful Shell executives world-wide, is considered
> by far the most crucial in predicting management poten-
> tial, particularly in the early stages of a career. [P. 36]

Most business-policy/strategic management courses have as their primary objective the development of this quality in students. It is also not surprising that most well-known business schools have business policy/strategic management as a core course in their MBA programs.

Implications for Further Research

Future research on the areas studied and reported herein should entail a replication of the present study. Replication can do much in evaluating the value and generalizability of this study's findings. Further empirical work is needed to see if these results may be generalized to industrial firms classified as small businesses. The study's findings indicate the importance of the general administration function and especially the need for effective strategic planning systems. In small businesses the dichotomy between planning and doing is not always clear-cut, and routine activities tend to take a large proportion of top management time. Therefore, empirical identification of critical functions and critical key result areas can be very helpful to small business managers.

The functional approach to the study of grand strategy can be modified and applied to settings other than large industrial corporations. In every organization, there exist a number of functional tasks. Any research that helps identify critical functions and critical key result areas for a particular type of organization can be very fruitful. The functional approach to the study of grand strategy needs to be extended to other business and nonbusiness organizations.

Other variables should be incorporated into the study of strategic mixes of functions for effective implementation of grand corporate strategies. Such variables as performance, investment intensity, and others have been suggested or examined by other corporate strategy studies. For instance, it might be fruitful to empirically test the differences in the strategic mixes of functions for a particular grand corporate strategy when the firms are categorized into high and low performers. It might also be useful to replicate the study using a different measure of perceived environmental uncertainty to evaluate the generalizability of the findings pertaining to the influence of perceived environmental uncertainty.

In this study, the focus of the research was to identify the strategic mixes of functions for effective implementation of grand corporate strategies. The study's approach might be modified to identify the influence of different functions in the formulation of different types of grand corporate strategies.

More research of a longitudinal type is also needed in a study of this type, since the concept of strategy is essentially dynamic. It is extremely important to bear in mind that even for the same firm and even without a change in the grand corporate strategy, the same top manager may perceive the strategic mix of functions differently at two different points in time. Longitudinal research studies can be undertaken for a small sample of homogeneous firms to assess causality in the relationships being tested.

Finally, further empirical work also needs to be done to identify strategic mixes of functions for different strategies within a firm, for different business strategies within a division, and for different key result areas within a function. For large multiunit companies with tremendous diversity, strategic planning needs to be analyzed as a multilevel process, the purpose of which is determined at each hierarchical level by the perceptions that the managers have of their task. According to Berg (1963), "For the purpose of corporate long range planning, a large, multiunit company cannot usefully be regarded as a single economic unit with a single set of interests" (Heau 1976, p. 19).

CONCLUDING STATEMENTS

To conclude, this research has made a contribution to the study of corporate strategy. It has integrated different concepts from corporate strategy literature and organizational theory and behavior literature in a coherent manner and has empirically studied certain relationships. The study has also contributed to the research methodology in the field of corporate strategy. It is important to note that research in corporate strategy is, for the most part, in embryonic stages. The major purpose of any research should be to add to existing knowledge in the area. It is believed that this research has provided evidence for further theoretical and empirical research, utilizing the strategic functional mix approach in the area of corporate strategy; it has also provided several implications for organizational practices.

Finally, this research emphasizes the importance of grand strategy over all the other organizational variables analyzed.

APPENDIX A

A CHECKLIST OF
FUNCTIONALLY GROUPED
KEY RESULT AREAS
RELEVANT TO
INDUSTRIAL FIRMS

A. General Administration

   1. Attracting and retaining well-trained and competent top managers
   2. Achieving a better overall control of general corporate performance
   3. Ability to perceive new business opportunities
   4. Simultaneous and continuous emphasis on efficiency (productivity) and innovation in patterns of firm's products, markets, technology, and management
   5. Developing and communicating a corporate identity, corporate mission and objectives, a corporate creed, and a grand corporate strategy—a unified sense of direction and a sense of common purpose to which all members of the organization can relate
   6. Ability to unify conflicting opinions, improve coordination, and enhance effective collaboration between key executives; generate enthusiasm and motivate sufficient managerial drive for growth and profits
   7. Developing a more effective company-wide strategic planning system for planned overall corporate development. Maintaining and enhancing the management depth by ongoing training and development programs for
   8.   a. Domestic operations
   9.   b. Overseas operations
  10. Need for greater international orientation at senior and middle management levels
  11. Increased participative decision making at senior and middle management levels
  12. Increased use of management by objectives and "responsibility accounting" reporting systems to facilitate joint goal-setting and self-evaluation of performance. Assuring and rewarding better judgment creativity and imagination in decision making at
  13.   a. Top management levels
  14.   b. Lower management levels
  15. A more extensive and effective use of quantitative techniques in decision making
  16. A more extensive and cost-effective computer system emphasizing richness, timeliness, flexibility, and accessibility of information for managerial decision making
  17. Ability and courage to identify and undo past strategic blunders (for example, by divestment)
  18. Ability to participate and be effective in industry organization and project a corporate image of an enlightened industry leader and a responsible corporate citizen worldwide

B. Production/Operations

19. Considering relocation of present production facilities in terms of opportunity costs of the existing sites

20. An ongoing plant modernization program to keep the efficiency of equipments comparable to those of the major competitors

21. Developing more flexibility in using facilities for different products and changing demand levels

22. Establishing production facilities overseas

23. A good trade-off between expanding capacity and increased subcontracting

24. An improved balancing of equipment capacities

25. Increased automation of production processes

26. Improved plant layout, workflow, and work environment

27. More efficient and reliable multiple-source material procurement

28. Reduced subcontracting and more extensive backward vertical integration

29. Owning and controlling (captive subsidiary) sources of raw materials

30. Measuring and controlling performance of purchasing, material handling, and traffic functions as effectively as production or sales performance

31. More effective equipment maintenance and replacement policies

32. Increased computerization and decentralization of production control systems for better control of quality, cost, and time

33. Improved materials and inventory control

34. Improved industrial engineering capabilities

35. Improved energy efficiency of production processes and equipments

36. Reduced air, noise, and other pollution and greater compliance with industrial health and safety regulations

37. Improved production-incentive systems for workers

38. Preparing employees for technological changes

C. Engineering and R&D

39. Improvement in basic research capabilities

40. Improvement in applied research and new product development capabilities

41. Value analysis for improving present products and developing and using alternative or substitute raw materials

42. Improved process engineering with an added emphasis on energy efficiency

43. Better overall management of and increased productivity from R&D expenditure by matching explicit R&D objectives and strategies with present and proposed product-market domain

44. Better cost control through shorter R&D investment payback time

45. Using multidisciplinary task forces or project teams for effective coordination between R&D operations and marketing (research)

46. National and international reputation for scientific and technological leadership

D. Marketing

47. Increased corporate commitment to the marketing concept
48. Improved marketing research and information systems
49. Widening the customer base by intensive market penetration and development
50. Developing overseas markets
51. Ability to secure large business contracts from governments and other large customers
52. Developing new products in new markets
53. Improved customer service
54. Exploring and developing fundamental new ways of providing services which are exclusive and customer oriented
55. More effective use of different pricing strategies
56. More novel and effective sales promotion and advertising campaigns
57. Effective and result-oriented control of marketing costs
58. Widening the distribution networks and improved distributor relations
59. Establishing and maintaining an efficient product distribution system
60. Stricter control over credit and collections
61. Improved product management
62. Developing more efficient and effective product-line policy for product additions and deletions
63. Maintaining a highly trained, motivated, vigorous, and dynamic sales organization

E. Finance

64. Improved bond ratings and common stock market performance
65. Maintaining a steady growth of earnings and improving the health of earnings

66. Providing a competitive return to shareholders through effective dividend policies even under price regulations
67. Improving financial public relations in general and stockholder relations in particular
68. Lower cost of equity capital and borrowings
69. Sound capital structure allowing flexibility to raise additional capital as needed
70. Strong working capital position allowing flexibility to raise short-term capital at low cost
71. Efficient and effective working capital management
72. Effective tax management
73. Ability to manage foreign investment risks of inflation and exchange losses
74. Effective capital expenditure evaluation procedures that would encourage taking risks with commensurate returns for new business opportunities in order to attain growth objectives
75. Extensive application of return-on-investment techniques and periodic monitoring of product-cum-market profitability
76. Effective financial, cost, and managerial accounting systems
77. Efficient, effective, and independent internal auditing system with tremendous top management backing

F. Personnel

78. Effective relations with trade unions
79. Effective and efficient personnel policies for hiring, training, promotion, compensation, and employee services
80. Ability to attract and retain high quality employees through the corporate image of a model employer
81. Optimizing employee turnover (neither too high nor too low)
82. Increased employee motivation and job satisfaction
83. Stimulating and rewarding creativity and innovativeness in employees
84. Achieving more effective two-way communication
85. Reliance on promotion from within
86. Maximum utilization of employee skills and competencies
87. Installing incentive performance reward systems
88. Periodical restructuring of organization structure to thwart empire-building tendencies
89. Effective grievance procedures
90. Stimulating more employees at all levels to continue to educate themselves to remain abreast of developments in their fields

G. Public and Government Relations

91. Ability to influence national policy in the industry
92. Effective relationships with relevant regulatory bodies
93. Better relations with consumer groups
94. Better relations with environmental groups
95. Better relations with local community
96. Better relations with minority groups
97. Ability to maintain satisfactory governmental relations with local, state, federal, and foreign governments
98. Devising better and newer ways of educating people in favor of the company
99. Promoting business and management ethics

APPENDIX B

COVER LETTERS AND QUESTIONNAIRE USED IN THE PILOT STUDY

There is usually an underlying logic behind the development of a business organization over time—a logic we call "corporate strategy." It is a grand design which includes but need not be expressed in terms of the microeconomics surrounding the engineering, manufacturing, and marketing of each of the firm's products. As a Chief Executive, you are most concerned with your firm's grand corporate strategy. Your experience provides you with a vision of what the separate things you observe (in your company) might constitute and a trained mind to carry out effective syntheses. However, the development of a systematized body of knowledge in the field of corporate strategy for training young managers has not yet come close to matching its crucial importance to the survival and growth of contemporary business organizations.

At the Oklahoma State University, we are currently engaged in corporate strategy research designed to develop a profile of key result areas (strategic factors) in different organizational functions that are crucial to effective implementation of different grand corporate strategies. We believe that the findings of this study would be useful and applicable to both the teaching and practice of management. However, we realize that without your active support and your approval of your company's participation we would not be able to obtain the requisite information.

We would appreciate it if you would have two senior company executives (familiar with your firm's overall operations and its overall business environment) complete the enclosed two identical copies of our questionnaire independently of each other and return the questionnaires in the enclosed, self-addressed, stamped envelopes as soon as possible. We assure you that no personal questions are asked nor is any proprietary information requested. The information supplied by your company's two executives will be kept in the strictest confidence and will appear only in aggregate statistical form. The important findings of the study will be made available to all participating firms upon request.

Thank you very much for your time and cooperation.

Sincerely,

Michael A. Hitt
Associate Professor of Management
Project Director

K. A. Palia
Research Analyst

July 18, 1978

CORPORATE STRATEGY QUESTIONNAIRE
FOR SENIOR EXECUTIVES

(to be filled out by a senior executive familiar with his/
her firm's overall operations and its overall business
environment)

The attached questionnaire is being administered to a select sample
of firms as part of our research study on corporate strategy. The
main objective of this study is to develop a profile of key result areas
(strategic factors) in different organizational functions that are crucial to effective implementation of grand corporate strategies in different types of firms. We believe that senior corporate executives
like you are the most knowledgeable people to provide meaningful insights on corporate strategies and therefore your support and cooperation are vital to the success of this study.

The questionnaire is designed to gather information about various aspects of your firm and its environment. No personal questions are
asked nor is any proprietary information requested. We hope that
the time spent by you in completing the questionnaire would be worth-
while. The information supplied in this questionnaire will be kept in
the strictest confidence. This research study does not necessitate individual case studies of participating firms; we are interested in using
the information in aggregated form only and hence your anonymity is
guaranteed.

May we request you to kindly complete the questionnaire and return it
in the attached self-addressed stamped envelope as soon as possible?
If you would like to give us any advice regarding this study, we would
be most happy to receive it. In particular, your comments or suggestions with respect to question wording, response structure, relevance to your firm, any notable omissions, etc. , would be most wel-
come. The important findings of the study will be made available to
all participants upon request.

Thank you very much for your time and cooperation.

Michael A. Hitt   K. A. Palia
Associate Professor of Management   Research Analyst
Project Director

September 7, 1978

About a month ago, we sent some questionnaires to you as a part of a research project on corporate strategies employed by different businesses. We have not received responses from your firm as yet. We realize that you and your colleagues have many demands. However, our project cannot be successful without participation from firms such as yours. We want you to know that we are dedicated to graduating students who can make strong contributions to Oklahoma's businesses. We are also dedicated to the development of effective extension efforts to our businesses in Oklahoma. This research project is designed to provide data which can help do both more effectively. We sincerely appreciate your support in this project. For your convenience, another set of questionnaires has been enclosed.

We would be sincerely appreciative of your having two senior company executives (familiar with your firm's overall operations and its overall business environment) complete the enclosed two identical copies of our questionnaire independently of each other, and return the questionnaires in the enclosed self-addressed stamped envelopes, as soon as possible. We assure you that no personal questions are asked nor is any proprietary information requested. The information supplied by your company's two executives will be kept in the strictest confidence and will appear only in aggregate statistical form. The important findings of the study will be made available to all participating firms upon request.

Thank you very much for your time and cooperation.

Sincerely,

Michael A. Hitt   K. A. Palia
Associate Professor of Management   Research Analyst
Project Director

MAH/KAP:rmm

Enclosure

September 7, 1978

CORPORATE STRATEGY QUESTIONNAIRE
FOR SENIOR EXECUTIVES

(to be filled out by a senior executive familiar with his/
her firm's overall operations and its overall business
environment)

The attached questionnaire is being administered to a select sample
of firms as part of our research study on corporate strategy. The
main objective of this study is to develop a profile of key result areas
(strategic factors) in different organizational functions that are crucial to effective implementation of grand corporate strategies in different types of firms. We believe that senior corporate executives
like you are the most knowledgeable people to provide meaningful insights on corporate strategies and therefore your support and cooperation are vital to the success of this study.

The questionnaire is designed to gather information about various aspects of your firm and its environment. No personal questions are
asked nor is any proprietary information requested. We hope that
the time spent by you in completing the questionnaire would be worth-
while. The information supplied in this questionnaire will be kept in
the strictest confidence. This research study does not necessitate individual case studies of participating firms; we are interested in using
the information in aggregated form only and hence your anonymity is
guaranteed.

May we request you to kindly complete the questionnaire and return it
in the attached self-addressed stamped envelope as soon as possible?
If you would like to give us any advice regarding this study, we would
be most happy to receive it. In particular, your comments or suggestions with respect to question wording, response structure, relevance to your firm, any notable omissions, etc., would be most wel-
come. The important findings of the study will be made available to
all participants upon request.

Thank you very much for your time and cooperation.

Michael A. Hitt   K. A. Palia
Associate Professor of Management   Research Analyst
Project Director

CORPORATE STRATEGY QUESTIONNAIRE
FOR SENIOR EXECUTIVES

Please answer <u>all</u> the questions. There are no right or wrong answers. The information supplied by the participants would be used in aggregated form only and hence your anonymity is guaranteed.

I. <u>GRAND CORPORATE STRATEGY</u>: This question is designed to ascertain the type of grand corporate strategy currently pursued by your firm. <u>The grand corporate strategy is the major plan of action for achieving the sales and earnings goals for the company as a whole (rather than a product, division or market segment)</u>. It is therefore the overall, predominant or master strategy of the firm. There are no good or bad, effective or ineffective, proactive or reactive strategies and contrary to popular belief, growth strategies are not the only effective or desirable strategies. Since each company is unique it has to evolve a grand strategy for attaining its corporate goals in the context of its unique organizational and environmental characteristics. Please remember, what is required is not the grand strategy you would prefer for the firm, but the one that is actually being pursued by your firm. <u>Check only one.</u>

[ ] A. <u>Stability Strategy</u>

Your firm continues to serve the customers in the same or similar product-market domain, has its main strategic decision focus on incremental improvement of functional performance, and continues to pursue the same or similar objectives, adjusting the level of achievement about the same percentage each year as it has achieved in the past.

(A Note for Items 2 and 3—Growth Strategies

Your firm is pursuing a growth strategy if it aims at increasing the level and/or scope of its product-market objectives upward in a significant increment, much higher than an extrapolation of its past achievement levels. Thus it not only strives at intensive growth of its current product line(s) but may also add new product lines which may or may not be related to its present business.)

[ ] B. <u>Internal Growth Strategy</u>

Your firm pursues <u>internal growth</u> strategy if your emphasis is predominantly on growth through <u>internal development</u> from <u>within</u> the company.

[ ] C. External Growth Strategy

Your firm pursues external growth strategy, if your emphasis is predominantly on acquisition of, or merger or joint venture with, other firms or divisions of firms.

[ ] D. Retrenchment Strategy

Your firm pursues retrenchment strategy if it tries to improve its performance by scaling down the level and/or scope of its product-market objectives by cutback in costs and by reducing the scale of operations by divestment of some divisions or units.

II. FIRM SIZE: What is your firm's annual sales revenue (inclusive of service and rental revenues but exclusive of non-operating revenues and excise taxes)? Check one.

[ ] A. $200 million and less
[ ] B. $201 million to $599 million
[ ] C. $600 million and over

III. CORPORATE DIVERSITY: To what extent is your firm diversified? Check one.

[ ] A. Single Business

95 percent or more of annual sales from one end product business.

[ ] B. Dominant Business

70 to 94 percent of annual sales from one end product business.

[ ] C. Related Business

Less than 70 percent of annual sales from one end product business and diversification primarily in concentrically related products (that is, similar markets or similar technology).

[ ] D. Unrelated Business

Less than 70 percent of annual sales from one end product business, and diversification unrelated to primary end product business (for example, a widely diversified multi-industry conglomerate).

IV. PERCEIVED ENVIRONMENTAL UNCERTAINTY: This question is designed to elicit from you your perception of the environmental conditions faced by your firm as a whole during the past 3 years. We are interested in your firm's overall relationships with various sectors of the external environment (for example, suppliers, customers, competitors). Specifically, we would like you to rate the characteristics or behavior of various sectors on the degree of their predictability, where 1 = highly predictable and 7 = highly unpredictable. The distinctions you make should be as precise as you feel you can make them.

	Predictable						Unpredictable
				(circle one)			
A. Suppliers of your raw materials and components							
1. Their price changes are	1	2	3	4	5	6	7
2. Quality changes	1	2	3	4	5	6	7
3. Design changes	1	2	3	4	5	6	7
4. Introduction of new materials or components	1	2	3	4	5	6	7
B. Competitors' actions							
1. Their price changes are	1	2	3	4	5	6	7
2. Product quality changes	1	2	3	4	5	6	7
3. Product design changes	1	2	3	4	5	6	7
4. Introduction of new products	1	2	3	4	5	6	7
C. Customers							
1. Their demand for existing products is	1	2	3	4	5	6	7
2. Demand for new products	1	2	3	4	5	6	7
D. The financial/capital market							
1. Interest rate changes							
a. Short-term debt	1	2	3	4	5	6	7
b. Long-term debt	1	2	3	4	5	6	7
2. Changes in financial instruments available							
a. Short-term debt	1	2	3	4	5	6	7
b. Long-term debt	1	2	3	4	5	6	7
3. Availability of credit							
a. Short-term debt	1	2	3	4	5	6	7
b. Long-term debt	1	2	3	4	5	6	7

	Predictable						Unpredictable

(circle one)

E. Government regulatory agencies

    1. Changes in laws or agency policies
       on pricing are   1 2 3 4 5 6 7

    2. Changes in laws or policies on
       product standards or quality   1 2 3 4 5 6 7

    3. Changes in laws or policies
       regarding financial practices   1 2 3 4 5 6 7

    4. Changes in labor (personnel)
       laws or policies   1 2 3 4 5 6 7

    5. Changes in laws or policies affect-
       ing marketing and distribution
       methods   1 2 3 4 5 6 7

    6. Changes in laws or policies on ac-
       ceptable accounting procedures   1 2 3 4 5 6 7

F. Actions of labor unions

    1. Changes in wages, hours, and work-
       ing conditions   1 2 3 4 5 6 7

    2. Changes in union security   1 2 3 4 5 6 7

    3. Changes in grievance procedures   1 2 3 4 5 6 7

V. RELATIVE STRATEGIC SIGNIFICANCE OF KEY RESULT AREAS
IN DIFFERENT ORGANIZATIONAL FUNCTIONS: This question is
designed to elicit from you your perceptions of relative strategic significance, of functionally grouped key result areas, to effective implementation of grand corporate strategy currently pursued by your
firm. A comprehensive list of key result areas (strategic factors)
grouped into seven functional categories has been prepared. Your
firm's performance in these different key result areas would determine how effectively your firm's grand corporate strategy would be
implemented; however the strategic significance of these key result
areas would differ. We would like you to evaluate each key result
area in terms of its strategic significance (to effective implementation
of your grand corporate strategy) based upon a seven-point rating
scale as shown below:

1 = Completely strategically insignificant
2 = Of very little strategic significance
3 = Of somewhat less than average strategic significance
4 = Of average strategic significance
5 = Of somewhat more than average strategic significance
6 = Of very great strategic significance
7 = Of the greatest strategic significance

Completely Strategically Insignificant					Of the Greatest Strategic Significance

(circle one)

A. General Administration

1. Attracting and retaining well-trained and competent top managers
    1 2 3 4 5 6 7

2. Achieving a better overall control of general corporate performance
    1 2 3 4 5 6 7

3. Ability to perceive new business opportunities and potential threats
    1 2 3 4 5 6 7

4. Developing and communicating a corporate identity, corporate mission and objectives, a corporate creed and a grand corporate strategy . . . a unified sense of direction and a sense of common purpose to which all members of the organization can relate
    1 2 3 4 5 6 7

5. Ability to unify conflicting opinions, improve coordination and enhance effective collaboration between key executives, generate enthusiasm and motivate sufficient managerial drive for growth and profits
    1 2 3 4 5 6 7

6. Developing a more effective companywide strategic planning system for planned overall corporate development
    1 2 3 4 5 6 7

7. Maintaining and enhancing the management depth by ongoing training and development pro-

	Completely Strategically Insignificant			Of the Greatest Strategic Significance
	(circle one)						
grams for both domestic and overseas operations	1	2	3	4	5	6	7
8. Increased use of MBO and "responsibility accounting" and increased participative decision making at senior and middle management levels	1	2	3	4	5	6	7
9. A more extensive and effective use of quantitative techniques in decision making	1	2	3	4	5	6	7
10. More extensive and cost-effective computer systems emphasizing richness, timeliness, flexibility and accessibility of information for managerial decision making	1	2	3	4	5	6	7

B. Production/Operations

11. An ongoing plant modernization program to keep the efficiency of equipment comparable to that of the major competitors	1	2	3	4	5	6	7
12. A good trade-off between expanding capacity and increased sub-contracting	1	2	3	4	5	6	7
13. Increased automation of production processes	1	2	3	4	5	6	7
14. Improved plant layout, work flow, and work environment	1	2	3	4	5	6	7
15. More efficient and reliable multiple-source material procurement	1	2	3	4	5	6	7
16. More effective equipment maintenance and replacement policies	1	2	3	4	5	6	7
17. Increased computerization and decentralization of production control systems for better control of quality, cost, and time	1	2	3	4	5	6	7

	Completely Strategically Insignificant					Of the Greatest Strategic Significance
		(circle one)				

18. Improved materials and inventory control   1 2 3 4 5 6 7

19. Improved industrial engineering capabilities   1 2 3 4 5 6 7

20. Reduced air, noise, and other pollution and greater compliance with industrial health and safety regulations   1 2 3 4 5 6 7

C. Engineering and R&D

21. Improvement in research and new product development capabilities   1 2 3 4 5 6 7

22. Value analysis for improving present products and developing and using more economical and easily available raw material substitutes   1 2 3 4 5 6 7

23. Improved process engineering with an added emphasis on energy efficiency   1 2 3 4 5 6 7

24. Better overall management of and increased productivity from R&D expenditure by matching explicit R&D objectives and strategies with present and proposed product-market domain   1 2 3 4 5 6 7

25. Using multidisciplinary task forces or project teams for effective coordination between R&D, operations, and marketing (research)   1 2 3 4 5 6 7

D. Marketing

26. Improved marketing research and information systems   1 2 3 4 5 6 7

27. Widening the customer base by intensive market penetration and development   1 2 3 4 5 6 7

	Completely Strategically Insignificant					Of the Greatest Strategic Significance
	(circle one)						
28. Ability to secure large business contracts from governments and other large, expecially overseas customers	1	2	3	4	5	6	7
29. More effective use of different pricing strategies	1	2	3	4	5	6	7
30. More novel and effective sales promotion and advertising campaigns	1	2	3	4	5	6	7
31. Widening and improving the product distribution networks and improving distributor relations	1	2	3	4	5	6	7
32. Developing more efficient and effective product-line policy for product additions and deletions	1	2	3	4	5	6	7
33. Maintaining a highly trained, motivated, vigorous, and dynamic sales organization	1	2	3	4	5	6	7

E. Finance

34. Improving bond ratings and common stock market performance	1	2	3	4	5	6	**7**
35. Providing a competitive return to shareholders through effective dividend policies even under price regulations	1	2	3	4	5	6	7
36. Improving financial public relations in general and stockholder relations in particular	1	2	3	4	5	6	7
37. Lower cost of equity capital and long-term borrowings	1	2	3	4	5	6	7
38. Sound capital structure allowing flexibility to raise additional capital for internal growth and acquisitions	1	2	3	4	5	6	7
39. Strong working capital position allowing flexibility to raise short-term capital at low cost	1	2	3	4	5	6	7

	Completely Strategically Insignificant					Of the Greatest Strategic Significance
			(circle one)				
40. Effective tax management	1	2	3	4	5	6	7
41. Ability to manage foreign invest-ment risks of inflation and ex-change losses	1	2	3	4	5	6	7
42. Effective capital expenditure evaluation procedures that would encourage taking risks with com-mensurate returns for new busi-ness opportunities in order to at-tain growth objectives	1	2	3	4	5	6	7
43. Extensive application of ROI tech-niques and periodic monitoring of product-cum-market profitability	1	2	3	4	5	6	7
44. Efficient, effective, and indepen-dent internal auditing system	1	2	3	4	5	6	7

F. <u>Personnel</u>

45. Effective relations with trade unions	1	2	3	4	5	6	7
46. Effective and efficient personnel policies for hiring, training, promo-tion, compensation, and employee services	1	2	3	4	5	6	7
47. Optimizing employee turnover (neither too high nor too low), through the corporate image of a model employer	1	2	3	4	5	6	7
48. Improved employee motivation, job satisfaction, and morale	1	2	3	4	5	6	7
49. Stimulating and rewarding creativ-ity in employees and installing in-centive performance reward systems	1	2	3	4	5	6	7
50. Effective grievance procedures	1	2	3	4	5	6	7
51. Stimulating more employees at all levels to continue to educate them-selves to remain abreast of develop-ments in their fields	1	2	3	4	5	6	7

	Completely Strategically Insignificant						Of the Greatest Strategic Significance
				(circle one)			

G. <u>Public and Government Relations</u>

52. Ability to influence national policy in the industry and to maintain effective relationships with relevant regulatory bodies   1   2   3   4   5   6   7

53. Better relations with special interest groups such as environmentalists, consumerists and others   1   2   3   4   5   6   7

54. Ability to maintain satisfactory relations with local, state, federal, and foreign governments   1   2   3   4   5   6   7

55. Improving overall corporate image   1   2   3   4   5   6   7

VI. <u>INDUSTRY</u>: What is the <u>principal industry</u> (representing the <u>largest</u> percentage of your total company sales) in which your firm operates? <u>Check only one.</u>

[ ] A. Consumer nondurable goods industry
[ ] B. Consumer durable goods industry
[ ] C. Capital goods industry
[ ] D. Producer goods (raw materials, components and supplies) industry

VII. <u>PRODUCTION SYSTEM</u>: What is the single, most predominant production system used in your firm? <u>Check only one.</u>

[ ] A. <u>Unit and small batch production</u> system (for example, production or fabrication of a single unit or a few units of products, like prototypes, custom pressings, special equipments, tools and dies, and so on, according to customer specifications).
[ ] B. <u>Large batch and mass production</u> system (for example, large batches of drugs, cans and bottles, mass production of automobiles, and so on).
[ ] C. <u>Continuous process production</u> system (for example, oil refining, chemicals, and so on).
[ ] D. None of the above (please specify)_____

VIII. ORGANIZATIONAL STRUCTURE: How would you characterize your firm's organizational structure? Check one.

[ ] A. Functional

An organization in which the major subunits deal with different organizational functions, like production, marketing and finance, rather than complete businesses. General management function is concentrated at topmost level and coordination and product-market performance are its primary responsibilities.

[ ] B. Functional with One or More Product Divisions or Subsidiaries

An organization that is basically functional, but which also has one or more separate product divisions or subsidiaries that report to top management (or in some instances to functional managers). The distinguishing characteristic of this hybrid form (which is neither wholly functional nor truly multidivisional) is that the general managers of the product divisions are organizationally on the same level or below the functional managers.

[ ] C. Product Division

An organization that consists of a central office and a group of quasi-autonomous divisions, each having the responsibility and resources needed to engineer, produce, and market a product or set of products.

[ ] D. Geographic Division

An organization that consists of a headquarters office and a group of operating divisions, each having the responsibility and resources needed to engineer, produce, and market a product or a set of products in a different geographic area.

[ ] E. Holding Company

An association of firms (or divisions) commonly owned by a parent corporation. Each firm is virtually autonomous and formal organization above the level of the individual firm is virtually nonexistent.

APPENDIX C

COVER LETTER AND SURVEY INSTRUMENTS USED TO COLLECT DATA FOR THE STUDY

November 27, 1978

At the Oklahoma State University, we are currently engaged in corporate strategy research designed to develop a profile of key result areas (strategic factors) in different organizational functions that are crucial to effective implementation of grand corporate strategies in different types of firms. We believe that the findings of this study will be useful and applicable to both the teaching and practice of management. A recently completed pilot study of a select sample of industrial firms in the southwest region has shown encouraging results; most of the senior executives participating in the pilot study have shown interest in receiving a summary of the important findings of the study. The enclosed questionnaires, designed to gather information about various aspects of your firm and its environment, are now being administered to a select sample of firms as a part of our nationwide study.

We would sincerely appreciate if you will spend a few minutes answering just one question listed in the chief executive officer's questionnaire and have any senior company executive (familiar with your firm's overall operations and its overall business environment) complete the senior executive's questionnaire and return them both in the enclosed, self-addressed, stamped envelope as soon as possible. We assure you that no personal questions are asked nor is any proprietary information requested. The information supplied in these questionnaires will be kept in the strictest confidence. This research study does not necessitate individual case studies of participating firms; we are interested in using the information in aggregated form only and hence, respondents may, if they so wish, remain anonymous. The important findings of this study will be made available to all participating firms on request.

In our opinion, senior corporate executives like you are the most knowledgeable people to provide meaningful insights on corporate strategies. We also realize that you and your colleagues have many demands and we deeply appreciate your support, which you would agree is essential to this project.

Thank you very much for your time and cooperation.

Sincerely,
Michael A. Hitt   K. A. Palia
Associate Professor of Management   Research Analyst
Project Director

MAH/KAP:vh

Enclosure

CHIEF EXECUTIVE OFFICER'S QUESTIONNAIRE

(to be filled out by the firm's chief executive officer)

GRAND CORPORATE STRATEGY: This question is designed to ascertain the type of grand corporate strategy currently pursued by your firm. The grand corporate strategy is the major plan of action for achieving the sales and earnings goals for the company as a whole (rather than a product, division, or market segment). It is therefore the overall, predominant, or master strategy of the firm. There are no good or bad, effective or ineffective, proactive or reactive strategies and contrary to popular belief, growth strategies are not the only effective or desirable strategies. Since each company is unique it has to evolve a grand strategy for attaining its corporate goals in the context of its unique organizational and environmental characteristics. Please remember, what is required is not the grand strategy you would prefer for the firm, but the one that is actually being pursued by your firm. Check only one.

[ ] 1. Stability Strategy

Your firm continues to serve the customers in the same or similar product-market domain, has its main strategic decision focus on incremental improvement of functional performance, and continues to pursue the same or similar objectives, adjusting the level of achievement about the same percentage each year as it has achieved in the past.

(A Note for Items 2 and 3—Growth Strategies:
Your firm is pursuing a growth strategy if it aims at increasing the level and/or scope of its product-market objectives upward in a significant increment, much higher than an extrapolation of its past achievement levels. Thus it not only strives at intensive growth of its current product line(s) but may also add new product lines which may or may not be related to its present business.)

[ ] 2. Internal Growth Strategy

Your firm pursues internal growth strategy if your emphasis is predominantly on growth through internal development from within the company.

[ ] 3. External Acquisitive Growth Strategy (including joint ventures)

Your firm pursues external growth strategy, if your emphasis is predominantly on acquisition of, or merger or joint venture with, other firms or divisions of firms.

[ ] 4. <u>Retrenchment Strategy</u>

Your firm pursues retrenchment strategy if it tries to improve its performance by scaling down the level and/or scope of its product-market objectives by cutback in costs and by reducing the scale of operations by divestment of some divisions or units.

SENIOR EXECUTIVE'S QUESTIONNAIRE

(to be filled out by a senior executive familiar with the firm's overall operations and its overall business environment)

This questionnaire is being administered to a select sample of firms as a part of our research study on corporate strategy. The questionnaire is designed to gather information about various aspects of your firm and its environment. Please answer all the questions. There are no right or wrong answers. The information supplied by the participants would be kept in the strictest confidence and used in aggregated form only, hence your anonymity is guaranteed.

I. FIRM SIZE: What is your firm's annual sales revenue (inclusive of service and rental revenues but exclusive of nonoperating revenues and excise taxes)? Check one.

[ ] A. $200 million and less
[ ] B. $201 million to $599 million
[ ] C. $600 million and over

II. INDUSTRY: What is the principal industry (representing the largest percentage of your total company sales) in which your firm operates? Check only one.

[ ] A. Consumer nondurable goods industry
[ ] B. Consumer durable goods industry
[ ] C. Capital goods industry (for example, industrial machinery and equipment)
[ ] D. Producer goods (raw materials, components, and supplies) industry

III. PRODUCTION SYSTEM: What is the single, most predominant production system used in your firm? Check only one.

[ ] A. Unit and small batch production system (for example, production or fabrication of a single unit or a few units of products, like prototypes, custom pressings, special equipments, tools and dies, and so on, according to customer specifications).
[ ] B. Large batch and mass production system (for example, large batches of drugs, cans and bottles, mass production of automobiles, and so on).
[ ] C. Continuous process production system (for example, oil refining, chemicals, and so on).
[ ] D. None of the above (please specify)_____

IV. CORPORATE DIVERSITY: To what extent is your firm diversified? Check one.

[ ] A. Single Business

95 percent or more of annual sales from one end product business.

[ ] B. Dominant Business

70 to 94 percent of annual sales from one end product business.

[ ] C. Related Business

Less than 70 percent of annual sales from one end product business and diversification primarily in concentrically related products (that is, similar markets or similar technology).

[ ] D. Unrelated Business

Less than 70 percent of annual sales from one end product business and diversification unrelated to primary end product business (for example, a widely diversified multi-industry conglomerate).

V. PERCEIVED ENVIRONMENTAL UNCERTAINTY: This question is designed to elicit from you your perception of the environmental conditions faced by your firm as a whole during the past 3 years. We are interested in your firm's overall relationships with various sectors of the external environment (for example, suppliers, customers, competitors). Specifically, we would like you to rate the characteristics or behavior of various sectors on the degree of their predictability, where 1 = highly predictable and 7 = highly unpredictable. The distinctions you make should be as precise as you feel you can make them.

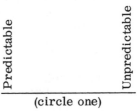

(circle one)

A. Suppliers of your raw materials and components

   1. Their price changes are   1 2 3 4 5 6 7
   2. Quality changes   1 2 3 4 5 6 7

	Predictable						Unpredictable
	(circle one)						
3. Design changes	1	2	3	4	5	6	7
4. Introduction of new materials or components	1	2	3	4	5	6	7

B. Competitors' actions

1. Their price changes are	1	2	3	4	5	6	7
2. Product quality changes	1	2	3	4	5	6	7
3. Product design changes	1	2	3	4	5	6	7
4. Introduction of new products	1	2	3	4	5	6	7

C. Customers

1. Their demand for existing products is	1	2	3	4	5	6	7
2. Demand for new products	1	2	3	4	5	6	7

D. The financial/capital market

1. Interest rate changes							
a. Short-term debt	1	2	3	4	5	6	7
b. Long-term debt	1	2	3	4	5	6	7
2. Changes in financial instruments available							
a. Short-term debt	1	2	3	4	5	6	7
b. Long-term debt	1	2	3	4	5	6	7
3. Availability of credit							
a. Short-term debt	1	2	3	4	5	6	7
b. Long-term debt	1	2	3	4	5	6	7

E. Government regulatory agencies

1. Changes in laws or agency policies on pricing are	1	2	3	4	5	6	7
2. Changes in laws or policies on product standards or quality	1	2	3	4	5	6	7
3. Changes in laws or policies regarding financial practices	1	2	3	4	5	6	7
4. Changes in labor (personnel) laws or policies	1	2	3	4	5	6	7

Predictable | Unpredictable

(circle one)

5. Changes in laws or policies affecting marketing and distribu-
   tion methods   1 2 3 4 5 6 7
6. Changes in laws or policies on ac-
   ceptable accounting procedures   1 2 3 4 5 6 7

F. Actions of labor unions

1. Changes in wages, hours, and
   working conditions   1 2 3 4 5 6 7
2. Changes in union security   1 2 3 4 5 6 7
3. Changes in grievance procedures   1 2 3 4 5 6 7

VI. <u>RELATIVE STRATEGIC SIGNIFICANCE OF KEY RESULT AREAS
IN DIFFERENT ORGANIZATIONAL FUNCTIONS</u>: This question is
designed to elicit from you your perceptions of relative strategic significance, of functionally grouped key result areas, to effective implementation of grand corporate strategy currently pursued by your
firm. A comprehensive list of <u>key result areas (strategic factors)</u>
grouped into seven functional categories has been prepared. Your
firm's performance in these different key result areas would determine how effectively your firm's grand corporate strategy would be
implemented; however the strategic significance of these key result
areas would differ. We would like you to evaluate <u>each</u> key result
area in terms of its strategic significance (to effective implementation
of your grand corporate strategy) based upon a seven-point rating
scale as shown below:

1 = Completely strategically insignificant
2 = Of very little strategic significance
3 = Of somewhat less than average strategic significance
4 = Of average strategic significance
5 = Of somewhat more than average strategic significance
6 = Of very great strategic significance
7 = Of the greatest strategic significance

	Completely Strategically Insignificant					Of the Greatest Strategic Significance
			(circle one)				

A. General Administration

    1. Attracting and retaining well-
trained and competent top
managers

            1 2 3 4 5 6 7

    2. Achieving a better overall con-
trol of general corporate performance

            1 2 3 4 5 6 7

    3. Ability to perceive new business
opportunities and potential threats   1 2 3 4 5 6 7

    4. Developing and communicating a
corporate identity, corporate mission and objectives, a corporate
creed and a grand corporate strategy . . . a unified sense of direction
and a sense of common purpose to
which all members of the organization can relate

            1 2 3 4 5 6 7

    5. Ability to unify conflicting opinions,
improve coordination and enhance
effective collaboration between key
executives, generate enthusiasm
and motivate sufficient managerial
drive for growth and profits

            1 2 3 4 5 6 7

    6. Developing a more effective com-
panywide strategic planning system for planned overall corporate
development

            1 2 3 4 5 6 7

    7. Maintaining and enhancing the
management depth by ongoing
training and development programs for both domestic and
overseas operations

            1 2 3 4 5 6 7

    8. Increased use of MBO and "re-
sponsibility accounting" and increased participative decision
making at senior and middle
management levels

            1 2 3 4 5 6 7

	Completely Strategically Insignificant					Of the Greatest Strategic Significance

(circle one)

9. A more extensive and effective use of quantitative techniques in decision making ... 1 2 3 4 5 6 7

10. More extensive and cost-effective computer systems emphasizing richness, timeliness, flexibility and accessibility of information for managerial decision making ... 1 2 3 4 5 6 7

B. Production/Operations

11. An ongoing plant modernization program to keep the efficiency of equipment comparable to that of the major competitors ... 1 2 3 4 5 6 7

12. A good trade-off between expanding capacity and increased sub-contracting ... 1 2 3 4 5 6 7

13. Increased automation of production processes ... 1 2 3 4 5 6 7

14. Improved plant layout, work flow, and work environment ... 1 2 3 4 5 6 7

15. More efficient and reliable multiple-source material procurement ... 1 2 3 4 5 6 7

16. More effective equipment maintenance and replacement policies ... 1 2 3 4 5 6 7

17. Increased computerization and decentralization of production control systems for better control of quality, cost, and time ... 1 2 3 4 5 6 7

18. Improved materials and inventory control ... 1 2 3 4 5 6 7

19. Improved industrial engineering capabilities ... 1 2 3 4 5 6 7

20. Reduced air, noise, and other pollution and greater compliance with industrial health and safety regulations ... 1 2 3 4 5 6 7

	Completely Strategically Insignificant						Of the Greatest Strategic Significance
				(circle one)			

C. Engineering and R&D

21. Improvement in research and new product development capabilities   1   2   3   4   5   6   7

22. Value analysis for improving present products and developing and using more economical and easily available raw material substitutes   1   2   3   4   5   6   7

23. Improved process engineering with an added emphasis on energy efficiency   1   2   3   4   5   6   7

24. Better overall management of and increased productivity from R&D expenditure by matching explicit R&D objectives and strategies with present and proposed product-market domain   1   2   3   4   5   6   7

25. Using multidisciplinary task forces or project teams for effective coordination between R&D, operations, and marketing (research)   1   2   3   4   5   6   7

D. Marketing

26. Improved marketing research and information systems   1   2   3   4   5   6   7

27. Widening the customer base by intensive market penetration and development   1   2   3   4   5   6   7

28. Ability to secure large business contracts from governments and other large, especially overseas customers   1   2   3   4   5   6   7

29. More effective use of different pricing strategies   1   2   3   4   5   6   7

30. More novel and effective sales promotion and advertising campaigns   1   2   3   4   5   6   7

	Completely Strategically Insignificant					Of the Greatest Strategic Significance
	(circle one)						

31. Widening and improving the product distribution networks and improving distributor relations

1 2 3 4 5 6 7

32. Developing more efficient and effective product-line policy for product additions and deletions

1 2 3 4 5 6 7

33. Maintaining a highly trained, motivated, vigorous, and dynamic sales organization

1 2 3 4 5 6 7

E. Finance

34. Improving bond ratings and common stock market performance

1 2 3 4 5 6 7

35. Providing a competitive return to shareholders through effective dividend policies even under price regulations

1 2 3 4 5 6 7

36. Improving financial public relations in general and stockholder relations in particular

1 2 3 4 5 6 7

37. Lower cost of equity capital and long-term borrowings

1 2 3 4 5 6 7

38. Sound capital structure allowing flexibility to raise additional capital for internal growth and acquisitions

1 2 3 4 5 6 7

39. Strong working capital position allowing flexibility to raise short-term capital at low cost

1 2 3 4 5 6 7

40. Effective tax management

1 2 3 4 5 6 7

41. Ability to manage foreign investment risks of inflation and exchange losses

1 2 3 4 5 6 7

42. Effective capital expenditure evaluation procedures that would encourage taking risks with commensurate returns for new busi-

	Completely Stratetically Insignificant				Of the Greatest Strategic Significance	

(circle one)

ness opportunities in order to attain growth objectives

1 2 3 4 5 6 7

43. Extensive application of ROI techniques and periodic monitoring of product-cum-market profitability

1 2 3 4 5 6 7

44. Efficient, effective, and independent internal auditing system

1 2 3 4 5 6 7

F. Personnel

45. Effective relations with trade unions

1 2 3 4 5 6 7

46. Effective and efficient personnel policies for hiring, training, promotion, compensation, and employee services

1 2 3 4 5 6 7

47. Optimizing employee turnover (neither too high nor too low), through the corporate image of a model employer

1 2 3 4 5 6 7

48. Improved employee motivation, job satisfaction, and morale

1 2 3 4 5 6 7

49. Stimulating and rewarding creativity in employees and installing incentive performance reward systems

1 2 3 4 5 6 7

50. Effective grievance procedures

1 2 3 4 5 6 7

51. Stimulating more employees at all levels to continue to educate themselves to remain abreast of developments in their fields

1 2 3 4 5 6 7

G. Public and Government Relations

52. Ability to influence national policy in the industry and to maintain effective relationships with relevant regulatory bodies

1 2 3 4 5 6 7

53. Better relations with special interest groups such as environmentalists, consumerists, and others

1 2 3 4 5 6 7

	Completely Strategically Insignificant						Of the Greatest Strategic Significance

(circle one)

54. Ability to maintain satisfactory re-
    lations with local, state, federal,
    and foreign governments   1 2 3 4 5 6 7
55. Improving overall corporate image   1 2 3 4 5 6 7

VII. ORGANIZATIONAL STRUCTURE: How would you characterize
your firm's organizational structure? Check one.

[ ] A. Functional

  An organization in which the major subunits deal with different
  organizational functions, like production, marketing and finance, rather than complete businesses. General management
  function is concentrated at topmost level and coordination and
  product-market performance are its primary responsibilities

[ ] B. Functional with One or More Product Divisions or Subsidiaries

  An organization that is basically functional, but which also has
  one or more separate product divisions or subsidiaries that
  report to top management (or in some instances to functional
  managers). The distinguishing characteristic of this hybrid
  form (which is neither wholly functional nor truly multidivisional) is that the general managers of the product divisions
  are organizationally on the same level or below the functional
  managers

[ ] C. Product Division

  An organization that consists of a central office and a group
  of quasi-autonomous divisions, each having the responsibility
  and resources needed to engineer, produce, and market a
  product or set of products

[ ] D. Geographic Division

  An organization that consists of a headquarters office and a
  group of operating divisions, each having the responsibility
  and resources needed to engineer, produce, and market a
  product or a set of products in a different geographic area

[ ] E. Holding Company

An association of firms (or divisions) commonly owned by a
parent corporation. Each firm is virtually autonomous and
formal organization above the level of the individual firm is
virtually nonexistent

REFERENCES

Ackoff, Russell L. 1970. A Concept of Corporate Planning. New York: Wiley Interscience.

Aguilar, Francis J. 1967. Scanning the Business Environment. New York: Macmillan.

Aldrich, Howard E. 1972. "Technology and Organizational Structure: A Reexamination of the Findings of the Aston Group." Administrative Science Quarterly 17: 26-43.

Allen, Stephen A., III. 1972. "Management Issues in Multidivisional Firms." Sloan Management Review 13 (Spring): 53-66.

Allison, Graham. 1971. Essence of Decision. Boston: Little Brown.

Anastasi, Anne. 1968. Psychological Testing. New York: Macmillan.

Anderson, Carl.R., and Frank T. Paine. 1975. "Managerial Perceptions and Strategic Behavior." Academy of Management Journal 18: 811-23.

Anthony, Robert N., and John Dearden. 1976. Management Control Systems: Text and Cases. Homewood, Ill.: Irwin.

Berg, Norman A. 1963. "The Allocation of Strategic Funds in a Large Diversified Industrial Company." Doctoral dissertation, Harvard Business School.

Bobbitt, H. Randolph, Jr., and Jeffrey D. Ford. 1980. "Decision-Maker Choice as a Determinant of Organizational Structure." Academy of Management Journal 5 (January): 15-23.

Bourgeois, L. J., III. 1980. "Strategy and Environment: A Conceptual Integration." Academy of Management Review 5 (January): 25-48.

Bowman, Edward H. 1974. "Epistemology, Corporate Strategy, and Academe." Sloan Management Review 15 (Winter): 35-50.

Buchele, Robert B. 1962. "How to Evaluate a Firm." California Management Review 5 (Fall): 5-17.

Burack, Elmer. 1975. Organizational Analysis: Theory and Applications. Hinsdale, Ill." Dryden.

Burns, Tom, and G. M. Stalker. 1961. The Management of Innovation. London: Tavistock.

Campbell, D. T., and D. W. Fisk. 1959. "Convergent and Discriminant Validation by the Multitrait-Multimethod Matrix." Psychological Bulletin 56: 81-105.

Cannon, J. Thomas. 1968. Business Strategy and Policy. New York: Harcourt Brace & World.

Chandler, Alfred D., Jr. 1962. Strategy and Structure: Chapters in the History of the American Industrial Enterprise. Cambridge, Mass.: MIT Press.

Child, John. 1975. "Managerial and Organizational Factors Associated with Company Performance—Part II. A Contingency Analysis." Journal of Management Studies 12: 12-27.

_____. 1972. "Organization Structure, Environment and Performance—The Role of Strategic Choice." Sociology 6: 1-23.

_____. 1970. "More Myths of Management Organization?" Journal of Management Studies 7: 376-90.

Claypool, P. L. 1975. "On a Friedman-Type Statistic for Paritally Ordered Preferences." Paper presented at the Joint Statistical Association meetings, St. Paul, March.

Cleland, David I., and William R. King. 1974. "Organizing for Long-Range Planning." Business Horizons 17 (August): 25-32.

Cronbach, L. J. 1970. Essentials of Psychological Testing. New York: Harper & Row.

Daft, Richard L., and Norman B. McIntosh. 1978. "A New Approach to Design and Use of Management Information." California Management Review 21 (Fall): 82-92.

Dewar, Robert, and Jerald Hage. 1978. "Size, Technology, Complexity and Structural Differentiation: Toward a Theoretical Synthesis." Administrative Science Quarterly 23: 111-36.

Dill, William R. 1958. "Environment as an Influence on Managerial Autonomy." Administrative Science Quarterly 2: 409-43.

Dun and Bradstreet Million Dollar Directory, 1978. 1978. New York: Dun & Bradstreet.

Duncan, Robert B. 1972. "Characteristics of Organizational Environments and Perceived Environmental Uncertainty." Administrative Science Quarterly 17: 313-27.

Emery, F. E., and E. L. Trist. 1965. "The Causal Texture of Organizational Environments." Human Relations 18: 21-32.

Emory, C. William. 1976. Business Research Methods. Homewood, Ill.: Irwin.

Ford, Jeffrey D., and John W. Slocum, Jr. 1976. "Size, Technology, Environment and the Structure of Organizations." Academy of Management Review 2: 561-75.

"The Fortune Directory of the 500 Largest U.S. Industrial Corporations." 1978. Fortune, May 8, pp. 238-63.

"The Fortune Directory of the Second 500 Largest U.S. Industrial Corporations." 1978. Fortune, June 19, pp. 170-96.

Fouraker, Lawrence E., and John M. Stopford. 1968. "Organizational Structure and the Multinational Strategy." Administrative Science Quarterly 13: 47-64.

Fox, Harold W. 1973. "A Framework for Functional Coordination." Atlanta Economic Review 23: 8-11.

Gaedeke, Ralph M., and Dennis H. Tootelian. 1976. "The Fortune '500' List—An Endangered Species for Academic Research." Journal of Business Research 4: 283-88.

Galbraith, J. K. 1967. The New Industrial State. Boston: Houghton Mifflin.

Galbraith, Jay R., and Daniel R. Nathanson. 1978. Strategy Implementation: The Role of Structure and Process. St. Paul, Minn.: West.

Gilmore, Frank F., and Richard G. Brandenburg. 1962. "Anatomy of Corporate Planning." Harvard Business Review 40 (November-December): 61-69.

Glueck, William F. 1976. Business Policy: Strategy Formation and Management Action. New York: McGraw-Hill.

Glueck, William F., and Robert Willis. 1979. "Documentary Sources and Strategic Management Research." Academy of Management Review 4: 95-102.

Godiwalla, Yezdi M. 1977. "Overall Corporate Strategy: The Functional Managements' Influence-Mix Approach." Ph.D. dissertation, Oklahoma State University.

Godiwalla, Yezdi M., Wayne A. Meinhart, and William D. Warde. 1979. Corporate Strategy and Functional Management. New York: Praeger.

Hake, Bruno. 1974. Hazards of Growth: How to Succeed through Company Planning. Translated by Peter G. Lucas. London: Longman Group.

Hall, Richard H. 1977. Organizations: Structure and Process. Englewood Cliffs, N.J.: Prentice-Hall.

Halpin, A. W. 1968. Theory and Research in Administration. New York: Macmillan.

Hambrick, Donald C., and Charles C. Snow. 1977. "A Contextual Model of Strategic Decision Making in Organizations." Academy of Management Proceedings, pp. 109-12.

Haner, F. T. 1976. Business Policy, Planning and Strategy. Cambridge, Mass.: Winthrop.

Heau, Dominique G. 1976. "Long Range Planning in Divisionalized Firms: A Study of Corporate Divisional Relationships." Doctoral dissertation, Harvard Business School.

Hickson, D. J., C. R. Hinings, C. A. Lee, R. E. Schneck, and J. M. Pennings. 1971. "A Strategic Contingencies' Theory of Intraorganizational Power." Administrative Science Quarterly 16: 216-29.

Hickson, D. J., D. S. Pugh, and Diana C. Pheysey. 1969. "Operations Technology and Organization Structure: An Empirical Reappraisal." Administrative Science Quarterly 14: 378-97.

Hill, William E. 1959. "Planning for Profits: A Four-Stage Method." California Management Review 1 (Spring): 28-38.

Hofer, Charles W. 1977. Conceptual Constructs for Formulating Corporate and Business Strategy. Case No. 9-378-754. Boston: Intercollegiate Case Clearing House.

_____. 1975. "Towards a Contingency Theory of Business Strategy." Academy of Management Journal 18: 784-810.

_____. 1973. "Some Preliminary Research on Patterns of Strategic Behavior." Academy of Management Proceedings, pp. 46-60.

Hofer, Charles W., and Dan Schendel. 1978. Strategy Formulation: Analytical Concepts. St. Paul, Minn.: West.

Howell, Robert A. 1970. "Plan to Integrate Your Acquisitions." Harvard Business Review 48 (November-December): 66-76.

Hrebiniak, Lawrence G. 1978. Complex Organizations. St. Paul, Minn.: West.

Jauch, Lawrence R., and Richard N. Osborn. 1981. "Toward an Integrated Theory of Strategy." Academy of Management Review 6 (July): 491-98.

Kast, Fremont E., and James E. Rosenzweig. 1973. Contingency Views of Organization and Management. Chicago: Science Research Associates.

Katz, Daniel, and Robert L. Kahn. 1966. The Social Psychology of Organizations. New York: Wiley.

Kendall, Maurice G., and William R. Buckland. 1971. A Dictionary of Statistical Terms. Edinburgh, England: Oliver and Boyd.

Kerlinger, Fred N. 1973. Foundations of Behavorial Research. New York: Holt, Rinehart and Winston.

Khandwalla, Pradip N. 1977. The Design of Organizations. New York: Harcourt Brace Jovanovich.

_____. 1976. "The Techno-Economic Ecology of Corporate Strategy." Journal of Management Studies 13: 62-75.

_____. 1974. "Mass Output Orientation of Operations Technology and Organization Structure." Administrative Science Quarterly 19: 74-97.

Kimberly, John R. 1976. "Organizational Size and the Structural Perspective: A Review, Critique, and Proposal." Administrative Science Quarterly 21: 571-97.

Kitching, John. 1967. "Why Do Mergers Miscarry?" Harvard Business Review 45 (November-December): 84-101.

Kloeze, H. D., A. Molenkamp, and F. J. W. Roelofs. 1980. "Strategic Planning and Participation: A Contradiction in Terms?" Long Range Planning 13 (October): 10-20.

Koontz, Harold. 1976. "Making Strategic Planning Work." Business Horizons 19 (April): 37-47.

Lawrence, Paul R., and Jay W. Lorsch. 1967a. "Differentiation and Integration in Complex Organizations." Administrative Science Quarterly 12: 1-47.

_____. 1967b. Organization and Environment. Boston, Mass.: Harvard Graduate School of Business Administration.

Li, L., and W. R. Schucany. 1975. "Some Properties of a Test for Concordance of Two Groups of Rankings." Biometrika 62: 417-23.

Lindsay, William M., and Leslie W. Rue. 1978. "Impact of the Business Environment on the Long-Range Planning Process: A Contingency View." Academy of Management Proceedings, pp. 116-20.

Litschert, Robert J., and T. W. Bonham. 1978. "A Conceptual Model of Strategy Formation." Academy of Management Review 3: 211-19.

Lorange, Peter. 1980. Corporate Planning: An Executive Viewpoint. Englewood Cliffs, N.J.: Prentice-Hall.

Lorsch, Jay W. 1973. "Environment, Organization, and the Individual." In Modern Organizational Theory: Contextual, Environmental, and Socio-Cultural Variables, edited by Anaut R. Negandhi. Kent, Ohio: Kent State University Press.

March, James G., and Herbert A. Simon. 1958. Organizations. New York: John Wiley & Sons.

Mason, R. Hal, Jerome Harris, and John McLaughlin. 1971. "Corporate Strategy: A Point of View." California Management Review 13 (Spring): 5-12.

Miles, Raymond E., and Charles C. Snow. 1978. Organizational Strategy, Structure, and Process. New York: McGraw-Hill.

Miles, Raymond E., Charles C. Snow, and Jeffrey Pfeffer. 1974. "Organization-Environment: Concepts and Issues." Industrial Relations 13: 244-64.

Miller, Richard D., and David J. Springate. 1978. "The Relationship of Strategy, Structure and Management Process." Academy of Management Proceedings, pp. 121-25.

Mintzberg, Henry. 1977. "Policy as a Field of Management Theory." Academy of Management Review 2: 88-103.

Moody's Industrial Manual. 1977. Vols. 1 and 2. New York: Moody's Investor Service.

Moody's OTC Industrial Manual. 1978. New York: Moody's Investor Service.

Murdick, Robert G. 1969. Business Research: Concept and Practice. Scranton, Pa: International Textbook.

_____. 1964. "The Long-Range Planning Matrix." California Management Review 7 (Winter): 35-42.

Murdick, Robert G., Richard H. Eckhouse, R. Carl Moor, and Thomas W. Zimmerer. 1976. Business Policy: A Framework for Analysis. Columbus, Ohio: Grid.

Murphy, David Charles. 1972. "Decentralization: The Effect of Technology." Academy of Management Proceedings, pp. 63-65.

Nachmias, David, and Chava Nachmias. 1976. Research Methods in the Social Sciences. New York: St. Martin's.

Newman, William H. 1971. "Strategy and Management Structure." Academy of Management Proceedings, pp. 8-24.

_____. 1967. "Shaping the Master Strategy of Your Firm." California Management Review 9 (Spring): 77-88.

Nunnally, Jum C. 1967. Psychometric Theory. New York: McGraw-Hill.

Paine, Frank T., and William Naumes. 1974. Strategy and Policy Formulation: An Integrative Approach. Philadelphia, Pa.: W. B. Saunders.

Perrow, Charles. 1970. Organizational Analysis: A Sociological View. Belmont, Calif.: Wadsworth.

Pitts, Robert A. 1977. "Strategies and Structures for Diversification." Academy of Management Journal 20: 197-208.

Pohl, Hermann H. 1973. "The Coming Era of the Financial Executive." Business Horizons 16 (June): 15-22.

Pugh, D. S., D. J. Hickson, C. R. Hinings, and C. Turner. 1969. "The Context of Organizational Structures." Administrative Science Quarterly 14: 91-114.

Quinn, James Brian. 1980. "Managing Strategic Change." Sloan Management Review 21 (Summer): 3-17.

Rawls, James R., Donna J. Rawls, and Raymond Radosevich. 1975. "Identifying Strategic Managers." Business Horizons 18 (December): 74-78.

Richards, Max D. 1978. Organizational Goal Structures. St. Paul, Minn.: West.

_____. 1973. "An Exploratory Study of Strategic Failure." Academy of Management Proceedings, pp. 40-46.

Rockart, John F. 1979. "Chief Executives Define Their Own Data Needs." Harvard Business Review 57 (March-April): 81-93.

Rumelt, Richard P. 1974. Strategy, Structure, and Economic Performance. Boston: Harvard Business School.

Salancik, Gerald, Jeffrey Pfeffer, and James Kelly. 1974. "A Contingency Model of Influence in Organizational Decision-Making." Academy of Management Proceedings, p. 55.

Schendel, Dan E., and Kenneth A. Hatten. 1972. "Business Policy or Strategic Management: A Broader View for an Emerging Discipline." Academy of Management Proceedings, pp. 99-102.

Schoeffler, Sidney, Robert C. Buzzell, and Donald F. Heany. 1974. "Impact of Strategic Planning on Profit Performance." Harvard Business Review 52 (March-April): 137-45.

Schucany, W. R., and W. H. F. Frawley. 1973. "A Rank Test for Two Group Concordance." Psychometrika 38: 249-58.

Scott, B. R. 1973. "The Industrial State: Old Myths and New Realities." Harvard Business Review 51 (March-April): 133-48.

Segal, Morley. 1974. "Organization and Environment: A Typology of Adaptability and Structure." Public Administration Review, May-June, pp. 212-20.

Smith, William, and R. Charmoz. 1975. "Coordinate Line Management." Working paper for Searle International, Chicago, February.

Snow, C. C., and D. C. Hambrick. 1980. "Measuring Organizational Strategies: Some Theoretical and Methodological Problems." Academy of Management Review 5: 527-38.

Sproul, Robert G., Jr. 1960. "Sizing Up New Acquisitions." Management Review 49: 80-82.

Standard & Poor's Register of Corporations, Directors and Executives. 1978. Vol. 1. New York: Standard & Poor's Corporation.

Starbuck, William H. 1976. "Organizations and Their Environments." In Handbook of Industrial and Organizational Psychology, edited by Marvin D. Dunnette, pp. 1069-1123. Chicago: Rand McNally.

Steiner, George A. 1969a. Strategic Factors in Business Success. New York: Financial Executives Research Foundation.

_____. 1969b. Top Management Planning. New York: Macmillan.

Steiner, George A., and John B. Miner. 1977. Management Policy and Strategy: Text, Readings and Cases. New York: Macmillan.

Stevenson, Howard H. 1976. "Defining Corporate Strengths and Weaknesses." Sloan Management Review 17 (Spring): 51-68.

_____. 1968. "Defining Corporate Strengths and Weaknesses." Doctoral dissertation, Harvard Business School.

Stone, E. F. 1978. Research Methods in Organizational Behavior. Santa Monica, Calif.: Goodyear.

Tavernier, Gerald. 1979. "Sure Signs of Success." International Management January, pp. 36-39.

Taylor, Bernard. 1973. "Introducing Strategic Management." Long Range Planning 6 (September): 34-38.

Terreberry, Shirley. 1968. "The Evolution of Organizational Environments." Administrative Science Quarterly 12: 590-613.

Terry, P. T. 1975. "Organizational Implications for Long Range Planning." Long Range Planning 8 (February): 26-30.

Thain, Donald H. 1969. "Stages of Corporate Development." Business Quarterly 34 (Winter): 33-45.

Thompson, Arthur A., Jr., and A. J. Strickland III. 1978. Strategy and Policy: Concepts and Cases. Dallas, Tex.: Business Publications.

Thompson, James D. 1967. Organizations in Action. New York: McGraw-Hill.

Tilles, Seymour. 1963. "How to Evaluate Corporate Strategy." Harvard Business Review 41 (July-August): 111-21.

Tuason, Roman V., Jr. 1973. "Corporate Life Cycle and the Evaluation of Corporate Strategy." Academy of Management Proceedings, pp. 35-40.

Vance, Jack O. 1970. "The Anatomy of a Corporate Strategy." California Management Review 13 (Fall): 5-12.

Vancil, Richard F., and Peter Lorange. 1975. "Strategic Planning in Diversified Companies." Harvard Business Review 53 (January-February): 81-90.

Ward, John L. 1976. "The Opportunity to Measure Strategic Variables: An Attempt to Quantify Product-Market Diversity." Journal of Economics and Business 28 (Spring-Summer): 219-26.

Weed, Stanley E., and Terence R. Mitchell. 1980. "The Role of Environmental and Behavioral Uncertainty as a Mediator of Situation-Performance Relationships." Academy of Management Journal 23 (March): 38-60.

Weick, Karl E. 1977. "Enactment Processes in Organizations." In New Directions in Organizational Behavior, edited by Barry M. Staw and Gerald R. Salanick, pp. 267-300. Chicago: St. Clair.

_____. 1969. The Social Psychology of Organizing. Reading, Mass.: Addison-Wesley.

Woodward, Joan. 1965. Industrial Organization: Theory and Practice. London: Oxford University Press.

Wrigley, Leonard. 1970. "Divisional Autonomy and Diversification." Doctoral dissertation, Harvard Business School.

INDEX

acquisitions: categories of, 11; or external acquisitive growth, 108–10

corporate diversity: effect of on the strategic significance of organizational functions, 112–14, 116, 137, 142–43; position of in the conceptual framework of the study, 73; Rumelt's specialization ratio for, 65–66; Wrigley's classification system of, 65–66

data analysis: by corporate diversity, 142; by firm size, 141; by industry, 143; by organizational structure, 145; by perceived environmental uncertainty, 146; procedures of, 106–8; by production system, 144

diversity, effect of on organizational structure and performance, 81–83

environment, types of, 24–27

environmental uncertainty, 26–37

environmental uncertainty (perceived): definition of, 69; effect of on the strategic significance of organizational functions, 140, 146; position of in the conceptual framework of the study, 73; as related to corporate strategy, 89

function, strategic: definition of, 83

functional specialization, 78

functions, organizational: effect of corporate diversity on, 142–43; effect of grand corporate strategy on, 136–41; effect of industry type on, 143–44; effect of organizational structure on, 145; effect of perceived environmental uncertainty on, 146; effect of production system on, 144–45; effect of size on, 141–42; identification of, 71; position of in the conceptual framework of the study, 73; relative strategic significance of, 133–34

grand corporate strategy: categories of, 61–62; definition of, 60–61; effect of on environment, organization, and management, 79–80; effect of various grand corporate strategies on the strategic significance of organizational functions, 136; position of in the conceptual framework of the study, 73

industry type: categories of, 68–69; effect of on the strategic significance of organizational functions, 137, 140; position of in the conceptual framework of study, 73

key result areas (strategic factors): definition of, 63; evaluation of in terms of strategic significance, 63–64, 130–31; as functionally grouped, 153–54

means-ends chain, 73

213

ABOUT THE AUTHORS

KYAMAS A. PALIA is currently a senior executive with Godrej and Boyce Mfg. Co. P. Ltd., Bombay, India, a very diversified and large corporation. He holds a B. Com. and M. Com. from Bombay University and a Ph.D. in Business Administration from Oklahoma State University. He is a certified chartered accountant (equivalent to C.P.A. in the United States) and is also a certified cost and works accountant in India. He has had work experience with a premier public accounting firm in Bombay. He has also taught courses in business policy at Oklahoma State University. At the university town of Stillwater he and Michael A. Hitt and R. Duane Ireland (both of Oklahoma State University) have collaborated on a major article to be published in 1982 in the Academy of Management Journal. Palia and Yezdi M. Godiwalla have worked very closely together previously at Godrej and Boyce and, subsequently, at Oklahoma State University in various projects in the strategic management-business policy area. In addition to scholarly empirical research, Palia has practical experience as a senior corporate executive. As such he has embraced diverse and challenging areas that encompass most spheres of complex organizational processes.

MICHAEL A. HITT is currently an Associate Professor of Management at Oklahoma State University. He earned his D.B.A. from the University of Colorado. Prior to his academic career he had several years industrial experience with Samsonite Corporation. He has also served as a consultant to a number of major firms, including IBM, Phillips Petroleum, Citibank, and Samsonite. Professor Hitt has authored and coauthored multiple articles for a variety of journals, such as the Academy of Management Journal, Journal of Applied Psychology, Strategic Management Journal, Human Relations, Personnel Psychology, Journal of Business Research, and Journal of Management. He is coauthor of two books—Effective Management (St. Paul: West, 1979) and Organizational Behavior: Applied Concepts (Chicago: SRA, 1981)—and author of another—Personnel Management: Jobs, People and Logic (Englewood Cliffs, N.J.: Prentice-Hall, forthcoming). His current research interests include examination of the relationships among grand strategy, industry, structure, and company performance; measurement of organizational effectiveness; and examination of ways to reduce industrial discrimination.

R. DUANE IRELAND is an Associate Professor of Management at Oklahoma State University. He earned his D.B.A. from Texas Tech University. His nonacademic work experience has been in the fields of manpower planning and programming and the development of innovative health-care delivery systems. He has served as a consultant to a number of firms and agencies, including Phillips Petroleum Company and the South Plains Association of Governments. Professor Ireland has been involved in multiple research projects. These efforts have resulted in articles in a wide range of journals, which include the Academy of Management Journal, Administrative Science Quarterly, Strategic Management Journal, Journal of Small Business Management, American Journal of Small Business, and Journal of Business Communication, among others. His current research interests center on the relationships among grand strategy, industry type, corporate structure, and firm performance. These relationships are being investigated in both large corporations and small business firms. Professors Ireland and Hitt are also assessing the differences between these sets of relationships for large and small firms.

YEZDI H. GODIWALLA is currently an Associate Professor in the Management Department at the University of Wisconsin-Whitewater. He holds a B.A. Honours and an M.B.A. in India and a Ph.D. in Business Administration from Oklahoma State University. He has published two scholarly books: Corporate Strategy and Functional Management and Strategic Management, Broadening Business Policy. He has published extensively with Wayne A. Meinhart and William D. Warde of Oklahoma State University. He has published numerous articles and presented papers at numerous professional conferences, mainly in the strategic management area, as well as in organizational theory and behavior, international management, and marketing management areas. At the University of Wisconsin-Whitewater, he has been conducting a series of strategic management research projects funded by the university's state research grants. He also has extensive senior executive experience with Godrej and Boyce Manufacturing Company P. Limited, Bombay, India, a large and diversified corporation.